Jews of a Saharan Oasis

In Memoriam of a Muslim and a Jew

(1) Hasan Ibrahim Gwarzo (d. *c.* 1990),
Grand Kadi of Kano State, Nigeria,
and scholar on Jews in Tamantit

(2) Nehemia Levtzion (1935–2003),
Israeli scholar on Islam in West Africa,
Colleague and Friend

Jews of a Saharan Oasis

Elimination of the Tamantit Community

John Hunwick

Markus Wiener Publishers
Princeton

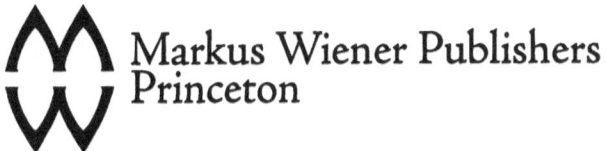

Second printing, 2018

For information write to:
Markus Wiener Publishers
231 Nassau Street, Princeton, NJ 08542
www.markuswiener.com

Library of Congress Cataloging-in-Publication Data

Hunwick, John O.
Jews of a Saharan oasis: elimination of the Tamantit community / John Hunwick.
p.cm.
Includes supplementary material translated from Arabic.
Includes bibliographical references and index.
ISBN-13: 978-1-55876-346-3 (paperback: alk. paper)
ISBN-13: 978-1-55876-345-6 (hardcover: alk. paper)
1. Jews—Algeria— Tamantit—History. · 2. Jews—Persecutions-Algeria—Tamantit. 3. Islam—Relations—Judaism. 4. Judaism-Relations—Islam. 5. Maghammad ibn Abd al-Kar (Algeria)—Ethnic relations. I. Title.
DS135.A3H86 2005
965'.7—dc22

2005032054

Contents

Glossary . . . vi

Preface . . . vii

Map: North and West Africa: Towns and Regions. . . . viii

1. Introduction: Next Year in Tamantit . . . 1

2. *Dhimmī*s in Islam . . . 5

3. Al-Maghīlī and His Views on the Jews . . . 11

4. *Fatwā* Judgments on the Jews of Tamantit . . . 33

5. Degradation and Diaspora of the Tamantit Jews . . . 61

6. Conclusion . . . 65

Appendix A: The *Qur'ān* on Jews . . . 69

Appendix B: Summary of *Fatwā*s of Ibn Zakrī and others . . . 71

Notes . . . 75

Bibliography . . . 85

Index . . . 89

Glossary

Amīr	Lit. "prince" or "chief"
Dhimmī	Lit. "protected [person]": a respected non-Muslim, either Christian or Jewish, living in Muslim territory
Fatwā	An authorized view, or collection of views, on a legal issue
Ḥadīth	A recognized saying of the Prophet Muḥammad
Jihād	Lit. "struggle", and often a battle against non-Muslims
Jizya	"Tribute": an annual tax-style payment to be paid by *dhimmī*s
Kanīsa	"Temple", i.e. a church or synagogue
Madh'hab	"School" of *sharīᶜa*
Muftī	A scholar who gives a *fatwā*
Qāḍī	"Judge" in Islamic law
Sharīᶜa	Traditional Islamic law

Preface

My first work on al-Maghılı was in the 1960s, principally on his responses to questions from the Songhay ruler Askiya *al-ḥājj* Muḥammad; but in studying the biography of al-Maghīlī, I came to discover his activity in Touat against the Jewish community of Tamantit. In the late 1960s the Nigerian scholar Hasan Ibrahim Gwarzo—then a graduate student at the School of Oriental and African Studies (University of London)—began research on the topic, completed as a thesis in 1972. Then, in 1985 and 1991, I was able to publish articles on the topic, and only recently decided that I should expand my earlier research so as to be able to produce and publish a whole book on the Jewish community of the Saharan oasis of Touat—having moved much of my interest into Saharan matters, with the setup of an Association of the Study of the Sahara (ASA) in the early 1990s. The present study also contains translations of two important, and relevant, Arabic texts of the fifteenth century; and for help in checking these, I am very grateful to Mohamed Eissa (formerly of Northwestern University).

It is now my hope that this book will increase interest in Saharan issues among Africanist scholars, making all such persons realize that "Africa" is not only the "black" sub-Saharan area of the continent, but that there have been, at least during the Islamic era, inter-connections between North Africa and Sudanic Africa across the Sahara. Hopefully it will also help promote interest in African matters among scholars of Judaism, despite the unhappy events for the Tamantit Jews that this book investigates.

John Hunwick
Professor Emeritus
Northwestern University
September 2005

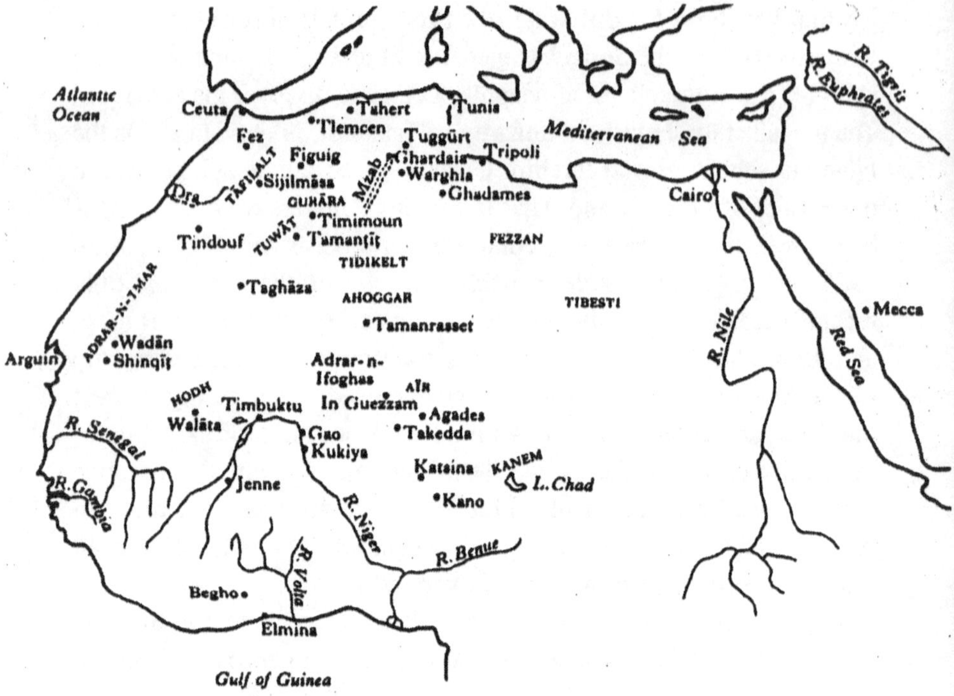

NORTH AND WEST AFRICA: TOWNS AND REGIONS

CHAPTER ONE

Next Year in Tamantit

When Capot-Rey, the French traveler through Algeria in the early 1950s, visited some north Saharan oases, he came across Jewish groups whose members, when Passover came, would often utter "Next year in Tamantit" instead of the more usual "Next year in Jerusalem". Normally, in celebration of Passover, faithful Jews express their wish to be back in their holy city of Jerusalem. However, these Saharan Jews evidently thought it appropriate to express a desire to be able to get back to the Saharan location from which they felt forced to flee after their synagogue was destroyed, and some of their community members killed, in the early 1490s.

Tamantit is a "fortified settlement,"[1] among many others that form the oasis of Touat along a normally dry wadi some 450–500 miles south of Tlemcen on the direct caravan route to Timbuktu. We do not know, for sure, when this oasis area was originally settled by Saharan nomads, and whether or not the first settlers were already Muslims, though likely they were, at least after the beginning of the second millennium C.E. In fact, a chronicle of Tamantit[2] states that it was founded by descendants of Yūsuf b. Tāshfīn, after the overthrow of the Almoravids, i.e. around 1150. As for Jewish settlers in Touat, it is evident that some were already settled there in the early fourteenth century, since there is a tombstone there inscribed in Hebrew and dated 1329 [C.E.].[3] More evidence of Jewish presence in the Sahara is evident from the fact that a map of the whole western Sahara area was produced in 1375 by two Majorcan Jews for Charles V of Aragon, which shows not only Sijilmasa and Dra "through [which] pass the merchants who travel to the land of the negroes of Guinea", but also Touat, Timbuktu, Gao, and Mali.[4] Such a map seems to show that Jews were already involved in trans-Saharan trade in the fourteenth century. In fact, Touat was like a junction for trade routes that came from the north, from Morocco to Tunisia, and those that came from the south, from Walata (in what is modern Mauritania) to Kano, or even the Bornu region (in what is now Nigeria). In 1447 a Genoese merchant, Antonius Malfante, visited Tamantit and observed the Jewish community there, remarking:

> There are many Jews who lead a good life here, for they are under the protection of the several rulers, each of whom defends his own clients. They also enjoy a very secure social standing. Trade is in their hands, and many are to be trusted with the greatest confidence.[5]

Jews had lived in North Africa since Roman times and, although some converted to Islam at various times and under various pressures, many sizeable Jewish communities continued to exist, as much in such great cities as Fez, Tlemcen, and Tunis as in the smaller towns and rural communities, especially in remoter areas such as the Atlas mountains and the Dra valley. Some also fled into the Saharan oases.[6] The Jews of the Maghrib suffered some persecutions under the Almohads in the 1140s and 1150s, but after the Marinids came to power in Fez in the mid-thirteenth century, a more tolerant atmosphere prevailed. At the same time, Almohad power in the Central Maghrib gave way to the dynasty of the Zayyānids (also known as the ᶜAbd al-Wādids) with its seat at Tlemcen, while the Ḥafṣids succeeded in Tunis. Under these dynasties, trade with Christian kingdoms of southern Europe began to flourish, not least (though perhaps quite surprisingly) between the Kingdom of Aragon and the city of Tlemcen through the intermediary of Majorca. Tlemcen itself was a key to the interior of Africa, being a major city relatively close to the Mediterranean Sea, but having well-developed commercial links with Sijilmasa and the Dra valley to the west, with Figuig and Touat to the south, and with Tuggourt and Warghla to the east.

The persecution of Jews in Castille, Aragon, and the Balearic Islands in 1391 led to a considerable exodus towards North Africa.[7] While this, and the spirit of the ongoing *reconquista*, effectively destroyed the great

Ibero-African commercial network, the influx of Jews with commercial and other skills had an enlivening effect on Jewish communities in the western and central Maghrib. Tlemcen's Jewish community was reconstituted by the Toledan rabbi, Ephraim Aln'Caoua, who obtained permission to bring Jews of the surrounding countryside into the city and to build a synagogue for them.[8] In the fifteenth century Tlemcen was considered a major Jewish spiritual center, the "Jerusalem of the west"[9]; its Jewish community prospered spiritually under the inspiration of rabbis of Iberian origin, and materially through its members' symbiotic relationship with the city's Muslim merchants.

By the fifteenth century, the Jewish element of Tlemcen's population was relatively large. Leo Africanus estimated its Jews at about 4% of the city's total population.[10] Muslim jurists there apparently had mixed feelings about this community and its conduct, as we shall see. The *qāḍī* Muḥammad al-ᶜUqbānī (d. 1467) strongly condemned the conduct of Jews who, so he said, dressed like Muslims, and went out on trading journeys in the company of Muslims, riding horses. He also condemned the Muslims who worked with them and were, apparently, prepared to risk their lives for their Jewish clients.[11]

So, with a large Jewish population in Tlemcen, involved in trans-Saharan trading, there was a clear connection with Touat. The condemnation of such Jewish activity may well have lain behind the condemnatory *fatwā* on the rights of Jews of Touat, produced by a Muslim scholar of Tlemcen, much of which can be found translated in Chapter Three below.

How this degradation of the Jews of Tamantit came about will be the topic of coming chapters, while translations of fundamental Arabic texts relating to this will also be given.

CHAPTER TWO

Dhimmīs in Islam

The term *dhimmī* (or collectively *ahl al-dhimma*) applies to non-Muslims, principally Jews and Christians, who were permitted to dwell in the "territories of Islam" (*dār/bilād al-Islām*) in return for payment of a special tax, the *jizya*,[12] on terms dictated by the Muslim authorities. These terms, much discussed by the Muslim jurisprudents, granted *dhimmīs* security of life and property—including, under certain circumstances, their places of worship—but imposed upon them many irksome and humiliating restrictions. Thus, while in theory, they enjoyed the protection of the law, they were, and were intended to be, second-class citizens—a minority preferably not to be seen, and certainly not to be heard. Their *dhimma* or "protection" was governed by a notional pact (*ᶜahd*), under which *dhimmīs* agreed not to fight against Muslims (except in self-defense), not to flout the regulations governing their behavior, and to pay the *jizya* and any other dues imposed upon them. Contravention of any stipulation in the pact could lead to their being put to death and their property being seized. These were not new ideas in the lands of the eastern Mediterranean, invented by the conquering Muslim Arabs in the mid-seventh century; indeed, at first, only security of lives, property, and places of worship, in exchange for the payment of *jizya,* constituted the elements of the pact, the so-called "Covenant of ᶜUmar", which details a long list of restrictions, being a much later fabrication. Many of these, in fact, reflected older regulations imposed by the Byzantines on Jewish communities, and then applied by Muslims to Jews and Christians alike. In particular, in Islamic law, restrictions on building or restoring places of worship had their counterpart in a Byzantine law of 423 C.E., which forbade Jews to construct new synagogues or to restore old ones.[13]

In the territories occupied by the Muslim Arabs in the first century of Islam, whether taken over by force of arms or through the peaceful submission of the local population, there was a need to keep the Muslims physically separate from the non-Muslim populations. At first, there may have been some fear that the newly converted Arabs might themselves be attracted to one of the religions of the conquered people; secondly, as members of the conquered populations began to convert to Islam, there was an even greater fear that some of them might abandon conversion. There was also, at least in the early period, a sense of Arab solidarity and superiority, which led the Arabs to establish new cities of their own—the *amṣār*—from which the conquered peoples were, at least in theory, excluded. It is fair to say, however, that we know very little about the actual conditions existing in conquered lands in the early years of the Islamic empire. The neat classification of lands and the laws governing them were rather the product of the minds of the jurists of the second century of Islam, who discovered, or invented, *ḥadīth*s and traditions, and projected back onto the early first century of Islam ideas that only crystallized in the mid- or late second century.

Although, at first, Muslims were only a tiny minority in a sea of non-Muslims in the conquered territories, and tolerance towards other religions was the only plausible policy, as time went on, and Muslims later came to be the majority, *dhimmī*s were more actively discriminated against and, in times of economic or political stress, were easily made scapegoats. However, while they were often humiliated and held in contempt, *dhimmī*s were also often made use of by Muslims, and their services were appreciated. In particular, some of their skills as craftsmen and physicians were in demand, and they could provide services such as money-lending and the working of precious metals, which were virtually prohibited to Muslims, owing to the strict law against interest (*ribā*). Sometimes Muslim rulers would use *dhimmī*s to undertake for them unpopular tasks, such as tax-collection, which only roused the ire of the taxed population,[14] exposing the *dhimmī* community, after the death of such a ruler, to violence and despoilment, or on other occasions to the breakdown of law and order. In rural areas, *dhimmī*s might live in a more or less servile condition, being forced to undertake labors such as latrine clearing, and being reviled, stoned, and segregated from the

Muslim population; on the other hand, they might live more or less integrated among the Muslims, enter into partnerships with them, and be protected by Muslim patrons. Everything depended upon the time and the place and, above all, on the prevailing economic conditions.[15]

Jews, however, were less well-regarded than Christians. This, no doubt, reflected what is to be found in a verse of the Qur᾿ān [5:82]:

> Thou wilt find the most hostile of people vis-à-vis those who believe [i.e. Muslims], to be the Jews and the idolaters. And thou wilt find the nearest of them in affection to those who believe to be those who say: "Lo! We are Christians". That is because there are among them priests and monks, and they do not display arrogance.

There were disputes between Muslims and Jews after the migration *(hijra)* of the Prophet Muḥammad to Yathrib, later known as Medina [*Madīnat al-nabī* = "the city of the Prophet"]. Jews formed a significant element of the population in that area before the *hijra*, and although a few of them accepted the Prophet's teachings and became Muslims, most remained as Jews, and were in disbelief of the divine authority of Muḥammad, and sometimes actively opposed him. As a result, most Jewish clans were expelled from Medina, and some of them migrated to the oasis of Khaybar, nearly one hundred miles north of Medina, a location that the Prophet Muḥammad finally attacked and took over—though, remaining there, the Jews were permitted to continue their agricultural work, but to act as land-serfs for the Prophet.[16]

Ultimately, if Jews did not take any active steps against Muslims, they were to be tolerated, since Judaism came to be seen as an earlier true faith—an "ancestor" of Islam, as was Christianity: both Moses and Jesus were believed to be "prophets of Allah" (as stated in the Qur᾿ān, 19:30 and 51), while Muḥammad was the final prophet, the "Messenger of God" (*rasūl Allāh*), and the Qur᾿ān the final true summary of Allah's messages for humankind. When most of what is nowadays called the Middle East was occupied by Arabian Muslims under the Caliph ᶜUmar b. al-Khaṭṭāb in the late 630s, many Jewish (as well as Christian) communities were brought under control. However, they were not forced to accept the Islamic faith, but were allowed to follow their own faiths and to retain their buildings of worship. The earliest agreement of conditions between a community of *dhimmīs* and dominant Muslims is what the Christians of Damascus are reported to have set up with the Caliph ᶜUmar b. al-Khaṭṭāb, after Arabian Muslim forces occupied that city (635–36); the agreement is known as:

The Covenant of ᶜUmar[17]

[The Christians said:] When you came to us, we asked you for security of our persons, our families, our property, and the people of our confession. We made to you condition upon ourselves [as follows]:

1. Not to build in our towns, or their environs, any new monastery, *kanīsa*,[18] *bīᶜa*,[19] or a monk's hermitage.
2. Not to repair those fallen into ruin.
3. Not to prevent any Muslim from staying in our churches at night, or by day.
4. To open our gates to passers-by and travelers.
5. To give passing Muslims residence for three nights, and feed them.
6. Not to lodge any spy in our houses or churches.
7. Not to conceal fraud towards Muslims.
8. Not to teach our children the Qurʾān.
9. Not to make manifest our religious law (*sharīᶜa*), and not to proselytise on behalf of it.
10. Not to prevent any one of our relatives from embracing Islam if he wishes to.
11. To treat Muslims with respect and to arrange seating for them in our gathering rooms, if they wish for it.
12. Not to resemble them in any clothing of theirs, such as a headcap (*qalansuwa*), or a turban or sandals, or in parting of the hair.
13. Not to speak as they do, and not to use their patronyms.
14. Not to use saddles when riding, not to gird ourselves with swords, and not to keep, or bear, arms of any sort.

15. Not to engrave our signet rings in Arabic.
16. Not to sell wine (*khamr*).
17. To cut our forelocks.
18. To stick to wearing our own clothing wherever we are.
19. To firmly fix girdles around our waists.
20. Not to display our crosses or our scriptures anywhere in the streets or markets of the Muslims.
21. Only to sound our [church-]bells gently.
22. Not to raise our voices when chanting in our churches in any place where Muslims dwell.
23. Not to parade on Palm Sunday or Easter.
24. Not to raise our voices [in lamentation] with our dead.
25. Not to display fires [i.e. candles] when [Muslims] are present in any place in the streets or markets of the Muslims.
26. Not to closely associate them with our deceased.
27. Not to take as slaves those who have been part of the booty of Muslims [in a *jihād*].
28. Not to overtake any houses of Muslims.

After this agreement reached Caliph ᶜUmar, he added two clauses, which he imposed upon them in addition to what they had imposed upon themselves:

1. Not to purchase any of the Muslims' captives.
2. Whoever among them deliberately strikes [a Muslim] has abrogated his pact.

While this original declaration of conditions was made by Christians, its restrictions were to be similarly applicable to other *dhimmīs*, such as Jews: not to construct worship buildings, not to openly display expressions of their faith, not to imitate Muslims in terms of appearance and behavior, and certainly not to disrespect or show opposition to Muslims. Also, in terms of not imitating Muslims, the question of riding similar animals as Muslims, with similar saddles, turned out to be a specific issue in relation to Jews around the Sahara.[20]

CHAPTER THREE

Al-Maghīlī and His Views on the Jews

Part I: Introduction to al-Maghīlī's treatise on the Jews

Muḥammad b. ᶜAbd al-Karīm al-Maghīlī, a Mālikī scholar, was born in Tlemcen around 1440, and after his years of study went to Tamantit,[21] where he took objection to the existence of a Jewish community with its own synagogue there. He may have initiated his anti-Jewish feelings through his experience of a Jewish community in his home city of Tlemcen.

The Jewish community of Tlemcen in the fifteenth century was relatively large,[22] including immigrants from Spain, who, like Muslims, had quitted their home cities when overtaken by Christians pushing down from the north of Spain. Muslim jurists there seem to have had mixed feelings about this community and its conduct. The *qāḍī* Muḥammad al-ᶜUqbānī (d. 1467) condemned the conduct of Jews, whom he accused of dressing like Muslims and making trading journeys in the company of Muslims, riding horses. He also condemned the Muslims who worked with them and were, apparently, prepared to risk their lives for their Jewish clients.[23] His grandfather, Qāsim b. Saᶜīd (d. 1450), also a *qāḍī* of Tlemcen, had issued a *fatwā* condemning the emigré "Jews of the hood" (*yahūd al-kabbūs*) for conspiring with the authorities to escape the formal payment of *jizya*.[24] Others, such as the *muftī* of Tlemcen, Ibn Zakrī (d. *c.* 1495), seem to have viewed them more sympathetically. He argued, for example, that the *dhimma* granted by Muslims to Jews was one and indivisible. If they moved from one part of the *dār al-Islām* to another, the rights they had in their first location were transferred to their new home, including the right to maintain a synagogue.[25] Nevertheless, the community was not always safe from depredations. It is said to have suffered in the year of al-ᶜUqbānī's death, 1467,[26] and again upon the death of the Zayyānid sultan Abū ᶜAbd Allāh Muḥammad in 921/1515–16, to such an extent that when Leo Africanus saw them (evidently, soon after the event), he considered them nearly all beggars.[27] Nothing appears to be currently known about this latter persecution, but it is likely that the *fatwā* of al-Tanasī on the synagogue of Touat, which also, more generally, deals with the rights and obligations of *dhimmīs*, and which is translated below in Chapter 4, had an overall adverse influence on Muslim-Jewish relations in Tlemcen.

As for the Jewish community of Tamantit, a description of it was given by a Genoese merchant, Antonius Malfante, who tried to do business there in 1447. Some of what he noted portrays a favorable attitude towards such Jews:

> There are many Jews who lead a good life here, for they are under the protection of the several rulers, each of whom defends his own clients. Thus they enjoy very secure social standing. Trade is in their hands, and many of them are to be trusted with the greatest confidence... [T]here are many rich men here. The majority, however, are very poor, for they do not sow, nor do they harvest anything, save the dates upon which they subsist.[28]

A somewhat different picture was presented by the *qāḍī* of Touat, ᶜAbd Allāh b. Abī Bakr al-ᶜAṣnūnī, who, in his letter to North African scholars, seeking a *fatwā* on the maintenance of the synagogue, claimed that the Jews of Touat were downtrodden and humiliated, mainly living in a single street (*darb*)[29] where their synagogue was situated among the houses.

Al-Maghīlī uses highly emotive language, describing Jews as "the enemies of God who insult Islam". They are the "personification of Iblīs"; they are "pigs and monkeys".[30] He provides scurrilous anecdotes designed to portray them as treacherous and filthy. He devotes only a few lines to the actual matter of the synagogues, and argues for their destruction, not through juristic offenses, but because the mere existence of synagogues in the lands of Islam is seen as an affront to the honor of Islam, and because any visible trace of a religion other than Islam is a contradiction of the humiliation and abasement in which the *dhimmīs* are constantly to be kept. He claims that consensus (*ijmā*ᶜ) forbids the building of any *kanīsa* in the territories of Islam, whether or not the land belongs to the *dhimmīs*.

He strongly argued against having positive attitudes towards Jews, seen as "unbelievers", especially because of their not acknowledging Muḥammad as the "Messenger of God". His contempt for Jews was expressed in some verses he wrote:

> Rise up, kill and enslave the infidels —
> Pigs, who care not for the name of Muḥammad.
> Rise up and kill the Jews; they are indeed
> The bitterest enemies who reject Muḥammad.
> Rise up and kill the Jews, as they were killed
> At Khaybar beneath the sword of Muḥammad.
> Rise up and kill the Jews and all of those
> Who fight for them; thus will you please Muḥammad.[31]

Summary of al-Maghīlī's treatise on the Jews.

This highly polemic and emotive work is addressed to "every Muslim man and woman", and its fundamental premise is that love of the Prophet—the sign of a true Muslim—necessitates hatred of his enemies. Whoever befriends or aids a Jew must be considered a *kāfir* (an "unbeliever"—a point on which Ibn Ghāzī disagreed). *Jizya* must be paid in a public ceremony of humiliation and abasement, which is an essential condition of *dhimmīs* being allowed to dwell in Muslim lands. It is forbidden for any *dhimmī* place of worship to be built in the occupied territories of Muslims and, if any governor gives permission for this, such permission is to be seen as null and void, and the building to be torn down. Al-Maghīlī asserted that Jews had been rebelling against the regulations governing their conduct, and the misdeeds of some of them have annulled the pact for all of them. Hence their men should be killed, their women and children enslaved, and their property seized.

The *qāḍī* of Touat, ᶜAbd Allāh b. Abī Bakr al-ᶜAṣnūnī, however, did not have any such opposition to the Jewish community or to its synagogue. So, in encountering al-Maghīlī's strong opposition, he sent a request for *fatwā*s on the issue to several North African *muftī*s; such a practice was followed by al-Maghīlī, who no doubt thought he could get support for his own views. The results of both their requests are discussed in the coming chapter.

Part II: Extracts of al-Maghīlī's *Miṣbaḥ al-arwāḥ fi usūl al-falāḥ*[32]

This is an epistle from the servant of God Most High, Muḥammad b. ᶜAbd al-Karīm b. Muḥammad al-Maghīlī al-Tilimsānī—may God look kindly upon him and upon all his beloved ones—through the exalted rank of our master Muḥammad—may God bless him and grant him and his Family and Companions peace—to every Muslim man and woman: Peace be upon you and the mercy and blessings of God, [as also His good pleasure and salutations].

Thereafter: One of the goodly folk asked me about the obligation for Muslims to steer clear of unbelievers, and about the necessity for "protected persons" to pay *jizya* and to receive humiliation and abasement; also about the hostile and oppressive behavior of the Jews of this age, and their revolt against the rulings and principles of the *sharīᶜa* through befriending men of might, or serving sultans.

I say—and God it is whose help is sought, and upon whom dependence is placed:

SECTION ONE
ON THE NECESSITY FOR MUSLIMS TO AVOID THE UNBELIEVERS

God the Exalted has said: "Vile women are for vile men, and vile men are for vile women. Good women are for good men, and good men are for good women". [Qur'ān, 24:26][33] Every type of person is more drawn to his own type than are all animals. Thus believers are friends, one to another; and whoso among you befriends them, then he is one of them.[34] On this I uttered the following verses:

> If a man draws nigh the good ones of his people
> And shuns the evil ones, then he is virtuous.
> If a man draws nigh the worst of his people
> And shuns the good ones, then he is vicious.
> Every man's comrade informs you about him.
> That is a clear matter among human kind.

The essence is that one brings no unbeliever close to himself or his relatives, nor employs him for jobs of his, and puts any money of his in his hands, unless one has no religion, no intelligence, and no manly virtue. As for the explanation of such a person having no religion, this is shown by rational proofs and legal texts. This is because God—Exalted is He—implanted it in the nature of every human being that He is not satisfied that any of His servants should be an intimate of any of His enemies, or that he should sever ties with one of His loved ones, whomever that might be. He made that generally [applicable] in all places over all time, such that no intelligent person would doubt that God—Exalted is He—would not be pleased that any of His worshippers would draw close to one of His enemies, or would sever ties with one of those whom He loves, since everything you see as a right of yours over your own slave, in terms of his severing ties with your enemies, and being in close touch with your beloved friends, and so forth, then God Most High has greater than that over you, since He—Exalted and Mighty is He—is the one who created you and regulated you, and in whose hand is that which benefits or harms you.

Then how could it please you to draw close an enemy of His or sever ties with one of His loved ones on account of some base desire of yours? You do not accept this from anyone linked to your side, so if you were to be aware that one of your loved ones had approached an enemy of yours, you would detest that of him and turn your heart away from him, not accepting any excuse from him until he distanced your enemies from himself.

"Thus God gives you examples"[35], your examples are from yourselves, "and what your right hands possess,[36] and what only the wise comprehend". "So ask the followers of the Remembrance, if you know not".[37] On this matter I said:

My beloved friend is he who is an enemy to my enemy, and
heals what is in my heart concerning foes,
Who exalts my view among other human beings, and
suppresses his own desire in regard to what I wish.

Every genuine believer must necessarily be harsh towards the unbelievers and compassionate towards the believers. The proof of this is that every believer must necessarily love the Prophet because of his saying—may God bless him and grant him peace: "None of you believes, unless I am dearer to him than his child and his father and all people."

Everyone who loves the Prophet must necessarily be with him, because of his saying—may God bless him and grant him peace: "A man is with whom he loves". And everyone who was with him, must necessarily be harsh towards unbelievers and compassionate with believers, because of the word of God Most High: "Muḥammad is the Messenger of God; and those who are with him are tough against the unbelievers, (but) compassionate with each other" [Qur'ān, 48:29]. He—Exalted is He—mentioned those who love His Prophet—may God bless him and grant him peace—with the words: "those who are with him" to draw attention to their great reward, and He characterized them as being harsh on the unbelievers, and compassionate to one another. So He mentioned those who love His Prophet—may God bless him and grant him peace—with the phrase "those who are with him", drawing attention to the greatness of their award; then He described them as being harsh upon unbelievers, and compassionate among themselves towards those who impose their love as a duty. Whoever interprets those [who are with him] as the Companions, does not intend to confine it to them or to specify them; indeed, he only mentions them, rather than others, so as to honor them and to praise them excessively, since they are the imams of the *umma*, and all the beloved ones have a preference for them. So the meaning is: Muḥammad is the Messenger of God, and those who are with him today are observing his *sunna*, and on the Day of Judgment will be in his party, and they are those who believe in him, who are characterized by love of him, who are harsh on his enemies, and compassionate to his *umma*. Hence *Qāḍī* Abū'l-Faḍl ᶜIyāḍ[38]—may God be pleased with him—said in the section [of his book] "On love of the Prophet"[39]—may God bless him and grant him peace—:

> And among [the implications] is his love for those who love the Prophet—may God bless him and grant him peace—and whoever is one of the members of his household (*āl baytihi*),[40] and his Companions, including the Emigrants (*al-muhājirīn*) and Helpers (*al-anṣār*),[41] and enmity towards those hostile to them and hatred for those who hate them..

The truth is that whoever loves something, loves everything that he [the Prophet] loves. This is the mode of conduct of the ancestors, even as regards permissible actions and personal desires (*shahawāt al-nafs*). Anas[42]—may God be pleased with him—when he saw the Prophet—may God bless him and grant him peace—stirring gourds around a large bowl, said, "From that day on I was always fond of the gourd". From them came his sympathy for the community (*umma*) of the Prophet—may God bless him and grant him peace—and his good advice to them, and his effort on behalf of their interests, and removal of harm from them, just as the Prophet—may God bless him and grant him peace—used to be kind and compassionate towards the believers.[43]

> Another sign is hatred for whomever God and His Messenger hated, and hostility towards those who are hostile to him [the Prophet], and avoiding whoever goes against his Sunna and makes innovations in his religion, and dealing heavily with all who conflict with his *sharīᶜa*.[44] God Most High has said: "You do not find a people who believe in God and the Last Day loving those who work against God and His Messenger, [even if they are their fathers or brothers or family members]" [Qurᵓān, 58:22].

> These are Companions of the Prophet—may God bless him and grant him peace—who killed their friends and fought their fathers[45] to please him—may God bless him and grant him peace. ᶜAbd Allāh b. Ubayy[46] said to him, "If you wish, I will bring you his head", meaning [the head of] his father.

Here ends what I took from him—may God be pleased with him.[47] One of my brethren [in God] informed me through his own chain of transmission, on the authority of Ibrāhīm al-Maṣmūdī, the leading personality *(quṭb)* of Tlemcen at that time, that he used to sit with a perfumer in his shop. One day he sought him out, as was his habit, and when with him he saw a Jew standing by him. So the *shaykh* fled off to his house. The perfumer got to know of that, and went to him and asked to be admitted to him, but the door was shut in his face and was not opened, and to him it was said; "A face with which you took interest in an enemy of God and His Messenger shall not be one with which you approach a beloved one of God and His Messenger, or anyone like that."

Similarly one of the brethren also informed me concerning *Ustādh*[48] Sīdī Hibat Allāh, a God-fearing scholar, that when he passed through Wādī Darᶜa,[49] and spent time there, he never went near the fortified settlement of the Banū Ṣubayḥ, because of the supporters *(awliyāʾ)* of the Jews. If he passed through the area for some affairs of his and came opposite their fortified settlement, he would bare his legs[50] and say to his companions: "Get out of the way! lest any anger falls upon supporters of the Jews and afflicts you together with them." He kept running with his companions until he was far from their fortified settlement.

Thus was the attribute of those loved by the Prophet—may God bless him and grant him peace—and how he acted over his enemies and all who were on their side, even if they were their fathers, their sons, their brothers, or their family. What made untruthful a people who assert that they believe in the Prophet—may God bless him and grant him peace—and love him, and, despite that, draw close to themselves and their families, enemies of his, and befriend people who are the most hostile to him, and who, because of them, break off relations with those who love him, to such an extent that today they seek refuge for Jews with them and fight the scholars over them? "Such are they who disbelieve in their Lord; such have *carcans*[51] on their necks; such are rightful owners of the Fire, they will abide therein" [Qur'ān, 13:5]. God—Exalted is He—said: "O you who believe, do not take Jews and Christians as friends. They are friends one to another. Whoever among you befriends them is indeed one of them. God does not guide wrongdoing people" [Qur'ān, 5:51]. God—Exalted is He—also said: "Tell the hypocrites that for them is a painful doom. Those who take unbelievers as friends in preference to believers, do they seek might from them? Surely, all might is God's" [Qur'ān, 4:138–39]. He who is Exalted also said: "You see many of them befriending those who disbelieve. Surely ill for them is what they send on before themselves, that God's wrath will be upon them, and in doom shall they abide. Had they believed in God and His Prophet, and what was revealed to him, they would not have taken them as friends; but many of them are evil-doers" [Qur'ān, 5:80–81]. He who is Exalted also said: "You shall not find a people who believe in God and the Last Day loving those who work against God and His Messenger, even if they are their fathers or brothers or family members" [Qur'ān, 58:22]. He who is Exalted also said: "Let not believers take unbelievers as friends in preference to believers. Whoever does that has no connection with God, unless you beware of them fully; and God Himself cautions you, and to God is the pathway." [Qur'ān, 3:28]. And there are Qur'ānic verses other than these. On this topic I uttered these [poetry] verses:

> In love for the Prophet, hatred of the Jews is necessary;
> Have regret for what has passed. Don't repeat it.
> Whoso befriends the enemies of the Prophet,
> How will it be for you in the grave,
> And resurrection into the flaming Fire?
> Who will plead on behalf of him if [the Fire] comes close
> To the face of him who gave satisfaction to the Jews?

As for proof of his having no intelligence, then it is through mental proofs and also legal texts. That is that the first mentality of a man is to bring his beloved ones close to the doors of his benefit, and that the greatest sectors of his misfortune are his enemies. It is up to every intelligent person to bring himself close to his beloved ones, and be as distant as possible from his enemies.

That being so, then it is he who distances himself, his family, and his wealth [from the unbelievers]; and he for whom this is unknown, then the donkey is more intelligent than him. If you know that, then he who does not keep himself, his family, his wealth, and all his activities, unknown to the unbelievers, then he is more ignorant than the donkey, since we have no enemy like the enemies of our Prophet, our master, and our intercessor, Muḥammad—may God bless him and grant him peace—especially the brethren of monkeys, for they are more severe in enmity towards us.

God—Exalted is He—has said: "Neither those who disbelieve among the People of the Scripture, nor the idolaters, love that there should be sent down unto you any good thing from your Lord. And God accords with His mercy whom He wills" [Qur°ān, 2:105]. Also: "They desire, were you to disbelieve as they do, that you could be on the same level." [Qur°ān, 4:89]. Again: "You will find those who show harshest enmity towards those who believe to be the Jews and those who are idolaters." [Qur°ān, 5:82]. Again: "Many of the People of the Scripture want to make you into unbelievers after your belief, out of envy emanating from themselves after the truth became clear to them." [Qur°ān, 2:109]. Also: "O you who believe, if you are submissive to a group of those who were given the Scripture, they will return you to being unbelievers after your belief" [Qur°ān, 3:99]. And so-on and so-forth in other verses.

One of the brethren—being a *qaḍī* in these territories—informed me that when he reached the territories and was made a *qaḍī* there, he employed a Jew in their activities. He said: "There came from me a slip in employing him, when I thought that his occupation was for his humiliation." Then he said: "He would act freely in my tasks, and show me sincere advice, so one day I gave him my clothes to wash, and I did not believe that he would be tardy [in doing the job]. So he was in front of me washing, and I watched until an urgent need called upon me; so I went and swiftly returned, finding him standing over my clothes and urinating on them. So I bound him and hit him, as God willed; and I became penitent in approaching all of God's enemies."

Also somebody told me that he saw a Jewish woman kneading

bread for a Muslim man, and taking a louse from her head and killing it between her fingernails, and then kneading again before washing her hands. Information on that is plentiful (and only a weak-sighted person would think of this as far-fetched),[52] and only one blind in mental perception does not expect worse than that. Have you not regarded the saying of Him who is Exalted: "O you who believe, take not for intimate friends other than your own folk, who would spare no pains to ruin you; they love to hamper you. Hatred is revealed through their mouths, but what their chests hide is greater. We have made clear to you the messages, if you have been understanding" [Qurʾān, 3:118].

As for an explanation of his being without manly virtue, this is through cognitive proofs and also legal texts. That is that everyone having high ambition and satisfying discretions must necessarily shun with his heart and limbs, and with his character, everyone who believes his defect, and signals his abuse, even if it were one of the most elderly of his people, like his father or his mother, and through this enmity and hatred multiply and grow between most relations, especially if everyone of a pair misleads the other in his *madh'hab*, and discredits him in religion. For this it is said:

> Affection from all enmity is hoped for,
> Except enmity of those hostile to you in religion.

We learned of the attack of unbelievers against us in religion, and their rumor about our religion, especially omnipotent fellows, for they are the most hostile folk towards us and our Prophet, our beloved one, our master, our lord, and our intercessor; and no one has less zeal than he who does not flee from them with his nature, his limbs, and his heart. How mean and disgraceful is he who allows them to draw close to him, since there is none of them who regards us without his actual tongue expressing hatred of us and abuse, and attacking us over our religion, to the extent that they forbid themselves our slaughtered animals and our foods and to cook in our pots, or eat out of our dishes. Worse than all that is their defamation of our Prophet and their derision of our prayer, and the way they oppose our master, our Prophet, our lord and intercessor [Muḥammad—may God bless him and grant him peace].

Thus, for that, God—Exalted is He, said: "O you who believe! Choose not My enemy and your enemy for friends. Do you give them friendship when they disbelieve in that Truth which came unto you?" [Qur'ān, 60:1]. He who is Exalted also said: "O you who believe! Do not take as friends those who took on the Scripture before you, or disbelievers who ridicule and degrade your religion. And be in awe of God, if you are true believers." [Qur'ān, 5:57].

Al-Qarāfī related that the caliph was angry with *Shaykh* Abū 'l-Walīd al-Ṭurṭūshī, and ordered that he be brought to his presence, being determined on his punishment. When the *Shaykh* entered his presence he saw a minister of the monks sitting opposite him, and—may God have mercy upon him—uttered these two verses:

> O king, whose generosity is sought by the aimer and desirer.
> He whom you honored on his account alleges this. He is a liar.

The caliph's anger increased when he heard these verses, so he ordered that the monk be withdrawn, and beaten and killed. The caliph approached *Shaykh* Abū 'l-Walīd [al-Ṭurṭūshī], talking to him, and he honored him, after having originally determined to do him ill. And this great goodness only came to the *Shaykh* and the caliph from their bringing to mind the hatred of the monk for the Prophet—may God bless him and grant him peace. So the *Shaykh*—may God be pleased with him—did not mind what was feared from the anger of the caliph and his killing. Hence God safeguarded him and gave satisfaction of him and, in honor of him, turned around the heart of the caliph and satisfied him. The Caliph—may God have mercy on him—did not mind what reversed him over the *Shaykh* from his love of him. Hence God safeguarded him against himself, and loved him, and purified him against the approach of an enemy of God and His Messenger. And he guided him, after taking control of him. Hence, it is obligatory for every believer to procure hatred for all unbelievers of our Prophet—our lord, our beloved one and intercessor—and to call to mind the greatness of their demands on us, and their challenge against us over our religion. Surely every unbeliever is a friend of the cursed Demon, the obvious enemy. So he overpowered him, and took on his brain and the contacts of his heart; and led him from his forehead, until he could not make any movement, or speak with any word, except through his opinion. So every believer at that time considered, through his belief of faith, that every Jew was no more than a demon in his own view; so he would flee from him with his religion, so he would not murder him through his closeness, in view of his not being aware of him. The closest thing of that is to reveal affection to him through some of his money, or his culture, so that some of his affection is plunged into his heart. So, by that he deserves the wrath of his Lord; or he would feed him from a game animal, or alcohol, or a corpse, or introduce to him interest in his earnings.

Note: The food produced by the [non-Muslim] Scripturist is of three types: the food of life-length (*ᶜumr*); the food of disbelief; and the food of deception. The food of life-length is what they made for themselves; to eat; this is their food, and it is lawful for us (to eat), though it is reprehensible, since Mālik[53]—may God be pleased with him—abhorred the eating of it for Muslims, whether they [the Scripturists] were *dhimmī*s or war people.[54]

Saḥnūn:[55] It is not eaten in their dishes until it is washed. The food of disbelief is what they produced for their *kanīsa*s and their feast-days,[56] and the likes of what is consistent with their deviation from the truth. This is not part of their food, but only a food of their disbelief, so it is not allowed to a Muslim, since it is one of the things that is offered to other than God, and aims at extreme disbelief in the Messenger of God. And they did not make food of deception for a Muslim, if he was among them, because they are people of disloyalty, betrayal, and penetrating enmity—so it is not permissible for a Muslim. So how can we be trustworthy in them over our foods; or how can we believe them that they performed slaughter and everything according to our rituals?

Because of that, it is not permissable for a Muslim to give authority to a disbeliever over brokerage, or sale, or purchase, or expenditure, because in that God Almighty has rights of which He seeks undertaking; and the rights of God Almighty cannot be trusted to a disbeliever. And everything they claimed to have slaughtered for us is a corpse; and all they allege to have spent for us is usury.

And because of that ᶜUmar b. al-Khaṭṭāb[57]—may God be pleased with him—ordered that they should not be butchers or treasurers, and that they should be carried out from all our markets.

And he said—may God be pleased with him—"Surely God has enriched Muslims through Muslims; so don't use unbelievers in any matter of your money." And in some of this portion is sufficiency to whomever guidance has been advanced from God. Only those with understanding have admonition, and God restores His grace to whomever He wishes, and God it is who makes correctness successful.

Section Two
On what is obligatory for *dhimmīs* in terms of tribute (*jizya*) and humiliation (*ṣaghār*)

God—Exalted is He—said: "Fight those who do not believe in God, or the Last Day, and do not forbid what God and His Messenger have forbidden, and, being of those given Scripture, do not adopt the religion of Truth, until they pay tribute readily, being brought low" [Qurᵓān, 9:29]. This is an order from God the Exalted of the necessity to kill Jews and Christians, and the sword will not be removed from their necks except on condition that they donate tribute by hand and are subdued. How is it appropriate that one of the enemies of the Master of the first and the last ones among the believers be left in the land of the Muslims until he submits tribute and submission stronger than burning with fire?

At that time it is appropriate that he be left with his wealth and family, since his humiliation through that is more curative than killing him and plundering his wealth. There is no means for us to leave alone any of the enemies of the chosen Prophet—may God bless him and grant him peace—in any of the villages, towns, or other locations, except for *jizya* and humility. As for *jizya*, it is money given, at the end of every year, by each adult male of them, free, powerful, and incorporative, as described by the *sharīᶜa*. Imposed upon them, and others like them, according to the injunction of [Caliph] ᶜUmar b. al-Khaṭṭāb—may God be pleased with him—was about eight mq.,[58] four of which are the basis of the *jizya*, and the other four following them from incomes, etc. Whoever is not met with oppression, gives all of it, if he is able to; and if he is met with oppression, he gives the basis of the *jizya*, and diminishes from it what follows it; that is if he did not violate any of the conditions upon *dhimmīs*. Otherwise nothing would be removed from him out of oppression until he fulfills all the conditions of a *dhimmī* upon him. And it is reduced from the frail one according to his weakness, so there is no limit to its least amount. And it is dropped from one who becomes a Muslim or is incapable of some of it. The form of its taking is that they are to be brought together on the day of its taking, in a well-known place, such as the market or something like it; and they attend its smallest and lowest place, standing on their feet, with *sharīʿa* officials [looking] over them, making them fear for themselves, until it appears to them and others that our aim is to manifest their humiliation by taking their money.

And they see that preference for us is to accept *jizya* from them and dispatch them. Then one individual after another of them is recruited to take hold of the *jizya*, and then he would be turned aside in clear rejection, seeing that through it he had got away from under the sword. Thus act beloved ones of the Master of the First and Last People on the disbelieving enemies of God; for might belongs to God, His Messenger, and the Believers.[59]

Taking hold of *jizya* is only done by commanders, or by one of the men of goodness, to the extent that taking it and spending it is in one hand, not in multiple hands. What other people take by themselves from their Jews is not just *jizya*. It is simply corruption on their appointment, and their disposal of the *jizya* is a continual booty. The conduct of just people in its disposal is to cover what must be covered in terms of fortress, arms, etc.; then gifts to the family of the Prophet—God bless him and grant him peace—and generosity to others; then possessions of the *ʿulamāʾ* and the believers. And everyone who has in his hand something of the affairs of religion, and benefits of the believers, according to the exertion of the administraters; then for the poor, according to their needs, so that the neediest is first until it covers all of them, if it can accommodate all of them. The remaining is to be distributed equally among all people—the poor, the rich and the devoid, and their patron. In an exceptional case, the imam, or whosever fulfills his absence, sees, with good intention, a wisdom in holding back this money, or part of it, for emergencies. If the money becomes scarce, and error and alarms become abundant—as is the case in this age—they will exercise on its expenditure, according to what can be done, since it is necessary to take *jizya* from *dhimmīs*, and to belittle them at all time, even if they are being iniquitous.

Oppressors have taken advantage [over others] by consuming *jizya*. God Almighty said: "God does not task a soul beyond its scope" [Qurᵓān, 2:286]. The Prophet—may God bless him and grant him peace—said: "If I command you in a matter, then do of it what you can." Hence, God Almighty made no condition over the taking of *jizya* from them, "until they pay it readily, being brought low". [Qurᵓān, 9: 29] As for humiliation, the occurrence is that they adhere to depravity and humility in their talk and actions and all their conditions, so that by that they will be taken over by every Muslim—male or female, free or slave. The first of what their juniors maintain over them in their religion is that they reject all that opposes the Muḥammadan *sharīᶜa*, even if it came from the Moses *sharīᶜa*, so that there does not appear to any Muslim anything of their prayer (*ṣalāt)*, or their recital, or their writings; and they do not praise in presence of a Muslim any of their own *ᶜulamāᵓ*, since the "message" is through religion, and jihad is based on religion. Since the contest between us and them over religion is from what He [God] Almighty said: "He it is who sent His Messenger with the guidance and the religion of truth, that He may cause it to prevail over all religion" [Qurᵓān, 48:28]. So if we overcome them following their religion, we prompt them to decline it. So they are diminished, even if, despite that, they possess hundreds of kilograms[60] of gold and silver, for when we overcome them hence, we overcome them in humility over religion and other matters. If we do not overcome them in that, and the rites of their disbelief remain active, their humility will be defective to the extent of what they celebrate of their religion, even if they give large amounts of gold and silver. Rather, acceptance of that from them rejects humility from them. Hence they should not be enabled to establish a *kanīsa* in any part of the Muslims' lands, even if they offer amounts of gold to cover the (surface of) the earth. How do believers sell any of the might of Islam in any way to enemies of the Prophet—blessing and peace be upon him—for this wreckage? "To God belong the treasures of the heavens and the earth, but the hypocrites comprehend not." [Qurʾān, 63:7]. "And bear unto the hypocrites the tidings that for them is a painful doom. Those who choose disbelievers for their friends instead of believers! Do they look for power at their hands? Lo! all power appertains to God" [Qurʾān, 4:138–39].

Nay, and by God, they shall have no power through it. Hence the Messenger of God—may God bless him and grant him peace—said: "Among you may not be raised any Jewish or Christian [item]", meaning a church or a synagogue. And he—may God bless him and grant him peace–said: "There should be no two [different] *qibla*s[61] in one region," and he also said: "Demolish monasteries and destroy synagogues." *Ḥadīth*s and traditions of the Prophet on that topic are numerous. ᶜUmar [b. al-Khaṭṭāb][62]—may God be pleased with him—said: "There is to be no *kanīsa* in the land of Islam." And he ordered that every *kanīsa* not in existence before Islam be destroyed, and he prohibited any *kanīsa* from being created. Society took on this matter, with no fear among all the scholars of the [Islamic] community. No creation of a *kanīsa* is lawful in any part of Muslim lands, nor is the setting up of any prayer house, or any relocation of theirs, even if they were to give gold for occupying the land. The territory they wanted to do that in was property of theirs, through a gift or through purchase, or anything else. If a sultan or a *qāḍī*, or anyone else, gave them permission for that, such permission was obliged to be refuted, and what they built destroyed, since no one's permission or judgment is to restrain the establishment of the truth and make change of what is forbidden, whoever is involved, and however long it took place: "Is it a judgment of the time of (pagan) ignorance that they are seeking? Who is a better than God for judgement to a people who have certainty (in their belief)?" [Qurʾān, 5:50]. The many evils in this age do not draw conclusions on the work of cities and the silence of the selected scholars; because the matter today and much previously is in the hands of sectarians and not the lords of piety. "Seek they other than the religion of God, when unto him submit whoever is in the heavens and on earth, willingly or unwillingly, and unto Him they will be returned" [Qurᶜān, 3:83]. Have you not considered *Shaykh* Abū 'l-Ḥasan al-Ashᶜarī, an imam of the Sunnis, who gave legal opinion that for a Muslim to build a *kanīsa* is disbelief? He said:

"There would be apostasy in his claim to be in need of that, as a willingness of infidelity (*kufr*)." Al-Qarāfī copied this from him in his book *al-Jam*ᶜ *wa'l-furūq*—that is clear.

Section Three
What Jews are up to in these times in most territories: boldness and tyranny, and rejection of *Shari*ᶜ*a* laws, with appointment of power commanders and service of the sultan

The section begins as follows:

> There is no doubt that as regards mentioned Jews, such as the Jews of Touat, Tījūrārīn, Tāfilālt, and Darᶜa, and many of the lands of Ifrīqiyā[63] and Tlemcen their blood, their wealth, and their women, became accessible, having no protection, since protection to keep the sword off them is the *sharī*ᶜ*a* protection of Islam, not pre-Islamic protection. They would only have *sharī*ᶜ*a* protection with the giving of *jizya* out of their hand, being submissive.

Following this comes the text of the document that was sent to [Caliph] ᶜUmar b. al-Khaṭṭāb by the Christians of Syria—a translation of which is to be found in chapter 2 above. Then al-Maghīlī continues as follows:

> So, when the document reached ᶜUmar—may God be pleased with him—he added to it [for them to say in their conditions]: "And we will not harm any Muslims. We condition that to you, over ourselves and the people of our faith, and we accept security over it. So, if we conflict with anything that we conditioned to you upon ourselves, and guaranteed, then we have no protection. And lawful for you, from us, is what is lawful to you on people of opposition and discord." ᶜUmar—may God be pleased with him—wrote to him [the author of the document] to carry out what they asked of, and

> adjoined to it two elements, making conditions upon them together with conditions they made upon themselves: "We will not purchase any of the Muslims' captives; and whoever [among us] deliberately strikes a Muslim has abrogated his pact."
>
> The ᶜ*ulama*ᵓ of every *madh'hab* depended on the laws relating to *dhimmī*s, except that they differed on what the treaty might attack over that. On the provision issue, Ibn Ḥazm said in [his] *Marātib al-Ijmā*ᶜ: "ᶜ*Ulamā*ᵓ differ over the infringement of the contract of the *dhimmī*, and the killing of one, and the capture of his family and his wealth, if he fails to observe any one of what we mentioned; that is the giving of four *mithqāl*s of gold at the end of every lunar year, and paying twelve *dirhams* for every *dīnār*; and not creating a *kanīsa*, or a monastery, a church, or a hermitage, and not renewing any such things destroyed; not to prevent Muslims from residing in their *kanīsa*s or churches at night or by day; and to make the doors of such buildings more spacious for the dwellers; and to hospitably receive Muslims who pass by them in threes; and not to accommodate a spy; and not to conceal an imposture for the Muslims; not to teach their children the Qurᵓān, but not to prevent them from entry into Islam."

The quotation of Ibn Ḥazm contains even more of the "Covenant of ᶜUmar". Then al-Maghīlī continues:

> One of the brethren informed me through his supportive information through the Imam al-Qaysī that a Jew used to serve [the Marīnid] Sultan Abū ᶜInān [of Fez]. From that he hence achieved contumacy, changing [interpretation of] something from the Qurᵓān for some young males ; that is that he passed on to a young man, asking for a formal opinion on the saying of Him, the Exalted: "Whoso seeks as religion anything other than Islam, it will not be accepted from

him" [Qurʾān, 3:84]. So the Jew said: Say: "Whoso seeks Islam as a religion, it will not be accepted from him". So the boy dropped the word *ghayr* [other than].

Al-Maghīlī includes poetry of his as he ends his writing on Jews:

To the Beloved Lord from the closeness of adherents of the
Jews I revealed
A people who ignored their religion, and justified the
religion of Jews.
That they quit their religion, and promoted the religion of
the Jews
Is sufficient disgrace of youths, and wickedness of the
source of their activity.
Would that they were to turn their back and reverse and ask
God's pardon
And conceal what they manifested of their victory to a
group of Jews.
Have they not seen how the Lord of mankind made
judgment over what had occurred?
How on earth does he whom Jews are pleased with get
pleasure?
No doubt it is not possible that truth is light in every
market.
The Copious Rewarding Lord gives it victory over
Christians and Jews.
O my God, through the Prophet, the selected one, the guide,
and the pious
And every celebrity and holy man is haughty over the
patrons of the Jews
Grace over them is shed away, and [therefore] succeed the
remains of their divine blessing,
And on their extermination open for them a gate to a fire of
fuel,
Except those who have sought [God's] pardon and have
restored what they have dismissed,

And make clear what they had concealed, until extremities
are made correct.
So have mercy to them over what has expired, and write to
them satisfaction from you.
And hurry with whomever of them judged in favor of
paradises of eternity.

Al-Maghīlī concludes that any failure by *dhimmīs* to observe every one of the conditions set up in the document submitted by Christians of Syria justifies an attack by Muslims. Naturally, al-Maghīlī cites much from the Qur°ān, so in Appendix A below are translations of all Qur°ānic verses referring to Jews.

CHAPTER FOUR

Fatwā Judgments on the Jews of Tamantit

In the 1480s Muḥammad b. ᶜAbd al-Jabbār al-Figīgī, a scholar from the oasis of Figuig, and a former pupil of al-Maghīlī, addressed a question to *Qāḍī* al-ᶜAṣnūnī concerning the legal status of the synagogues existing in several Saharan *quṣūr* (fortified villages), and more particularly the synagogue of Tamantit. He also posed questions relating to the conduct of Jews living among these Muslim communities.

Al-Figīgī's request for a *fatwā* from al-ᶜAṣnūnī may have been instigated by al-Maghīlī, who, knowing the *qāḍī*'s personal position on the question of the synagogue, wished to force him to take an official position and thus provoke a formal dispute. Certainly, al-Maghīlī came out with a forceful attack on al-ᶜAṣnūnī when his *fatwā* was promulgated, insinuating that he was to be considered an unbeliever (*kāfir*) or an Anti-Christ (*dajjāl*).

Al-ᶜAṣnūnī argued that, although the settlements of Touat had been established by the Muslims—a fact which in most views would debar *dhimmīs* from establishing any places of worship there—cogent reasons could be given to allow existing synagogues to remain. In the first place, no other scholar of Touat, throughout the ages, had ever ruled that they be demolished, and the local Arab chiefs (*al-khalāʾif*)[64] had sanctioned their existence from time immemorial. Despite the lack of an actual formal agreement, such continuing sanction had the legal weight of a pact. Secondly, it was likely that these Saharan Jews had emigrated from some other Muslim land, where they had had an agreement permitting them to maintain synagogues. He quoted a ruling of Ibn *al-Ḥājj* al-Fāsī (d. 1336) in support of the right to build a new place of worship following emigration, provided the *dhimmīs* concerned had in no way broken their pact. Both al-Maghīlī and al-Figīgī had, in fact, argued that, in addition to any other argument in favor of demolishing the synagogue, the Jews of Touat had broken their pact by attempting to put themselves on a par with Muslims socially, and by failing to pay *jizya* in the prescribed manner and amount.

Other views on the situation of Jews in Tamantit exist in views of jurists consulted by al-ʿAṣnūnī, the names and views of some of whom have been preserved in the great collection of *fatwās* of the Maghrib and Andalusia put together by Aḥmad b. Yaḥyā al-Wansharīsī, in *al-Miʿyār al-mughrib ʿan fatāwī ʿulamāʾ Ifrīqiyā wa 'l-Andalus wa 'l-Maghrib*. Among those who responded were: Aḥmad b. Muḥammad, known as Ibn Zakrī, *muftī* of Tlemcen (d. *c.* 1494); Abū Mahdī ʿĪsā b. Aḥmad al-Māwasī, *muftī* of Fez (d. 1491); Muḥammad b. Qāsim al-Anṣārī, known as al-Raṣṣāʿ, *qāḍī 'l-jamāʿa* and *muftī* of Tunis (d. 1489); and Abū Zakariyyāʾ Yaḥyā b. ʿAbd Allāh b. Abī 'l-Barakāt, *qāḍī 'l-jamāʿa* of Tlemcen (d. 1504). All of these, as may be discerned from the offices they held, were pillars of the Mālikī *madh'hab*, and in every way properly qualified to deliver a judicial opinion. Each of them, with varying qualifications, opposed the demolition of a place of worship built on land of which *dhimmīs* had lawful possession. A summary of their *fatwās* can be seen in Appendix B.

Ibn Zakrī ruled that although *dhimmīs* are forbidden to build new places of worship, this does not mean it is an obligation to demolish those already built and possessed. Existing *kanīsa*s should be left, even if new ones are forbidden. This applies to *dhimmīs* who have no pact. If they have a pact, and they move around within the lands of Islam, their pact remains and they should be allowed to build a new *kanīsa*. To demolish the synagogues would be an injustice (*ẓulm*); and injustice towards *dhimmīs* is not permissible.

The view of al-Mawāsī, the *muftī* of Fez, was that *kanīsa*s already in existence should not be demolished, as they may result from an ancient privilege granted to the *dhimmīs*, unless it can be shown that the *dhimmīs* had transgressed by building them. In fact, says he, the people concerned are *dhimmīs*, who are humble and abased, and no one has raised any objection to the synagogues over the years.

Abū Zakariyyā°, the *qāḍī'l-jamā*ᶜ*a* of Tlemcen, also held similar views, stating: "Anyone with the least intelligence, who ponders the facts of this case, will know that the synagogues may not be demolished, since warding off evil takes precedence over obtaining benefits. What evil could be greater than stirring up dissension and strife—which may lead to killing and plundering of property?"

Support for al-Maghīlī's views, however, came from the Tlemcen scholar whom he approached for a *fatwā*, Muḥammad b. ᶜAbd al-Jalīl al-TanasI—not himself a *muftī*, but more recognized as an historian.[65] He referred to al-Maghīlī's demand as follows. All following quotations were taken from *al-Mi*ᶜ*yār al-mughrib* of Aḥmad b. Yaḥyā al-Wansharīsī:[66]

> There has come to us from your district a question which runs as follows: "What do you say—may God give you success—on the question of Tamantit, the [chief] town of Touat, whose land the Muslims reclaimed by pumping out its waters, and by planting date palms and building fortified villages over a period of time? Then there came to them Jews, who settled with them in the aforementioned town, and established therein a new synagogue[67] to practice their religion. This has been the situation over time until the present day. Should this synagogue be demolished, even if they had owned the land on which it was built before it was constructed, having obtained it by purchase, or other means, from the Muslims;? Or should it not be demolished? Give us a *fatwā* about this through an unambiguous reply—and may you receive the reward. The Muslims are in a state of perplexity over this matter. If destruction of it is the true right, they would have demolished it without strife or discord. If the right is that it should be left standing, they would leave it so without strife. God it is who brings success. Peace be upon you and the mercy of God.

Al-Tanasī wrote very extensive responses, some principal elements of which are the following:[68]

Know—may God illuminate your spiritual vision and purify your inner essences of the pursuit of base inclination—that the *sharīᶜa* of Muḥammad abrogated every other religious law and cured sick hearts of every illness, since its suns came forth shining, and its proofs appeared in decisive fashion. Learned scholars undertook to preserve it, taking it upon themselves to defend it through the passage of time, concerning themselves with explaining the judgment to be given in the problem contained in the question, century after century, from the time of the Companions [of the Prophet] onwards. We shall cite to you from their pronouncements, which will leave no room for doubt, nor could anyone wish for anything further.

The fundamentals of this are *ḥadīth*s related on the authority of the Best of Messengers, and traditions transmitted, in their dependence, on the authority of the Companions and Followers, and believed in, in ancient and recent times, by Muslim scholars. Anas—may God be pleased with him—related that the Messenger of God, may God bless him and grant him peace, said: "Demolish monasteries and destroy churches." ᶜUmar b. al-Khaṭṭāb related that he [Prophet Muḥammad], may God bless him and grant him peace, said: "No *kanīsa* should be newly established in Islam[ic lands], nor should any that have been demolished be restored." Ibn ᶜAbbās, may God be pleased with him, related that he, may God bless him and grant him peace, said: "There is to be no emasculation in Islam, and no building of any *kanīsa*." Ibn Ḥibbān mentioned these *ḥadīth*s in the book he wrote on the regulations regarding *dhimmī*s;[69] similarly, Abū ᶜUbayd Qāsim b. Sallām in his *Kitāb al-amwāl*.[70] Both of these imams are in the same rank as the five celebrated imams of *ḥadīth*. Ibn ᶜAbbās also related that the Messenger of God, may God bless him and grant him peace, said: "There shall not be two *qibla*s in a single town (*balda*)". This was mentioned by Abū Dāwūd. Al-Baghawī[71] also reported a similar one with the words: "It is not fitting that there should be two *qiblas* in one single territory." Ibn al-Munāṣif quoted it in his book *al-Injād fī adāb al-jihād*,[72] using it as a proof concerning the issue of the question. Ibn Ḥabīb related on the authority of Ibn al-Mājishūn, who said: "I heard Mālik [b. Anas] say: 'The Messenger of God—may God bless him and grant him peace—said: "Neither any Jewish nor Christian one is to be raised amongst you'." And Mālik added: "He meant synagogues and churches." These *ḥadīths* are among the informations of his prophecy—may God bless him and grant him peace—since [their topic] is something he gave information on before it existed, so it was found to be like that.

As for the post-Prophetic traditions (*āthār*), it is related that ᶜUmar b. al-Khaṭṭāb—may God be pleased with him—said: "[There is to be] no *kanīsa* in the Abode of Islam." This was mentioned by Abū ᶜUbayd; and Sālim b. ᶜAbd Allāh related, on the authority of his father, that ᶜUmar b. al-Khaṭṭāb—may God be pleased with him—ordered that every *kanīsa* that had not been in existence before Islam should be demolished, and forbade that any [new] one should be created. Ibn Badrān, a contemporary of al-Bājī, mentioned this.

Writing of the Governor to ᶜUmar b. al-Khaṭṭāb when he made a settlement with the Christians of Damascus [p. 237]

When Ibn Ḥibbān quoted the preceding *ḥadīths* with his own *isnāds*, he said: "Abū Yaᶜla al-Mawṣilī told us as follows: Rabīᶜ b. Thaᶜlab said to us: 'Yaḥyā b. ᶜUqba b. Abī 'l-Ayzār related to us on the authority of Sufyān al-Thawrī and al-Rabīᶜ b. Nūḥ al-Suddī, on the authority of Ṭalḥa b. Muṣrif, on the authority of Masrūq, on the authority of ᶜAbd al-Raḥmān b. Ghunam, that he wrote to ᶜUmar b. al-Khaṭṭāb when he came to a peace agreement with the Christians of Damascus'."

In the name of God, the Merciful and Compassionate. This is the writing sent to the Servant of God ᶜUmar, the Commander of the Faithful, from the Christians of Damascus: "When you people reached us, we asked you for immunity for ourselves and our descendants, and for our wealth and for the people of our religious community. For you we made a condition on ourselves not to set up in our towns, or in their neighborhoods, a monastery, or a *kanīsa*, or a church, or a monk's hermitage; or to renew any of them demolished. And that we also do not prevent our *kanīsa*s from providing accommodation for any Muslim for a night or a day; or that we expand their doors for a pedestrian woman and a wayfarer; and that we give Muslims who pass through [the city] three nights of residence in *kanīsa*s and provide food for them. Nor should any spy be accommodated in any of our *kanīsa*s or dwellings; nor should we keep secret any oppression of Muslims, or teach our children the Qurʾān; or manifest our law, or summon anyone to it. Nor should we forbid anyone related to us from conversion to Islam, if he so wishes. And that we should respect the Muslims, and if they wish to be seated, we should rise from our seats, in honor of them. Nor should we imitate them in any of what they wear in headgear, turban, shoe pairs, or parting of the hair. Nor should we speak as they do, or use [sur]names of theirs. Nor should we ride on saddles, or take on swords, or adopt any kind of weapon, or carry it with us. Nor should we engrave on our seals in Arabic; nor should we sell wine. And we should detach the bows of our chiefs, and stick with our clothing as we were, and fasten girdles around our waists, and not display our crosses and bibles in any roadway or market of the Muslims, and only ring our [church-]bells softly, and not raise our voices in recitation in our *kanīsa*s in the presence of any Muslims; nor should we bring out our crosses or our *yāghūth*;[73] nor raise our voices with our deceased. Also not to display [candle-]fires with them in any of the roadways or markets of the Muslims; nor to come close to them with our deceased. And not to take any slave hit with arrows of Muslims, or overtake residences of Muslims.

The official text of the "peace agreement", forming the basis of what Muslims were to expect from communities of *dhimmīs*, the so-called "Covenant of ᶜUmar", was translated in chapter 2 above. After that Al-Tanasī makes more arguments as follows [p. 238]:

> We have given it in its entirety because of scholars' use of it as an authority, whenever they discussed any of its clauses. What concerns the [present] question is only the first clause of it. What is aimed at in the preceding *ḥadīths* and traditions is that the lands ruled over belong to the Muslims, because of the way he used such expressions as "in Islam" or "among you", addressing the Muslims, or by the expression "in the Abode of Islam". The general can be applied to the particular, and it includes, according to this explanation, areas laid out by the Muslims—the subject of the question—and what the Muslims took possession of by force; but it does not include lands taken under peace agreement, since they belong to those who made the peace agreement rather than the Muslims. This explanation was handed down from Ibn ᶜAbbās, may God be pleased with him. Abū ᶜUbayd and Ibn Ḥibbān, whose wording is cited, related on the authority of ᶜIkrima that he said: "Ibn ᶜAbbās was asked; 'May non-Arabs (*ᶜajam)* build anything new in the cities *(amṣār)* of Arabs?' He replied: 'In any city founded by the Arabs, non-Arabs may not build a church or display wine to the public gaze, or bring a pig into it, or sound the church bell (*nāqūs*) within it'."

Aspects of Settlement in Islam [p. 239]

Following the statement of Ibn ᶜAbbās, Abū ᶜUbayd gave the following commentary on his words "settled by the Arabs":

> There are various definitions of 'settlement' (*tamṣīr*):
>
> (i) a locality whose inhabitants convert to Islam, such as al-Madīna, al-Ṭāᵓif and the Yemen;

(ii) any uninhabited area that the Muslims plan out and settle in, such as Koufa and Basra;

(iii) any town taken by force that the imam does not see fit to return to those from whom it was taken. These are original cities (*amṣār*) of the Muslims in which there is no way for *dhimmīs* to make public any of their religious regulations (*sharāʾiᶜ*)—for example setting up places of worship, allowing fermented liquor or pigs to be seen in public, or sounding the church-bell. As for the place where there is a way for them to do such things, there would not have been any peace they had compromised on, so it would not be denied of them.

On this point Ibn ᶜAbbās said: "It behoves the Muslims to keep their part of the agreement. This includes lands such as Ḥijr, al-Baḥrayn, Ayla and Dūmat al-Jandal."[74] This statement of Ibn ᶜAbbās, which provided such detail, is what the scholars of the Islamic world (*al-umma*) have used as an authority from earliest times until the present. They considered it a commentary on the preceding Prophetic *ḥadīths*.[75]

Similar statements have come down from the scholars of the generation of the Followers. Ibn ᶜAbbās related on the authority of al-Nakhāʾī, who said: "A document of [Caliph] ᶜUmar b. ᶜAbd al-ᶜAzīz came to us when we were in enemy [non-Muslim] territory, in which he said: "Do not destroy any synagogue, church or fire-temple, which was the subject of a peace agreement. And do not [allow them to] construct any new synagogue, church, or fire-temple (*bayt nār*)." Abu ᶜUbayd related a similar thing. Ibn Badrān said: "The doctrine (*madh'hab*) of ᶜUmar b. ᶜAbd al-ᶜAzīz was that no church or synagogue, either old or new, should be left in the Abode of Islam." Al-Ṭurṭūshī[76] reported it in the same way. What is meant by this is [houses of worship] other than those in their contract at the time of their peace agreement, because it has already been reported that he said: "Do not demolish what they made a peace agreement about." Also because of Abu ᶜUbayd's report that Ḥassān b. Mālik mentioned a complaint against the non-Arabs (*ᶜajam*) of Damascus, to ᶜUmar b. ᶜAbd al-ᶜAzīz, over a *kanīsa* which one of the *amīrs* had apportioned to him as a fief. ᶜUmar said: "If it is one of the fifteen in their pact, you have no right to it." ᶜAbd al-Razzāq related on the authority of Muᶜammar that he heard al-Ḥasan al-Baṣrī say [p. 240]: "It is *sunna* that *kanīsas*, both old and new, should be demolished in the occupied cities *(amṣār)*", i.e. those that were not in their contract. It is related of Ṭāʾūs al-Yamānī that he said: "It is not fitting for the House of Mercy to be in a house of punishment. Abū ᶜUbayd said: "He meant that *kanīsas* should not co-exist with mosques in the cities of the Muslims. This was derived from the saying of him, [the Prophet Muḥammad], upon whom be blessing and peace: "There shall not be two prayer niches *(qibla)* in a single town." The statement of Ṭāʾūs ought not to be interpreted as a [total] interdiction. What Abū ᶜUbayd said, regarding the cities of the Muslims, indicates that land subject to a peace agreement is excluded.

What came in regard to *kanīsas*, on the authority of the scholars of the Islamic world, who came after the Companions and the Followers, is is very plentiful. Of it we shall mention what was reported in the Mālikī and other *madh'habs*, from which may be realized the reliance that all have on the preceding traditions and *ḥadīths*.

In the section on "Wages and Hiring" *(al-juᶜl wa 'l-ijāra)* in the *Mudawwana* [we read]: "Mālik said: "The *dhimmīs* may not establish new *kanīsas* in a land of Islam, unless they are given authority." Ibn al-Qāsim said: "They may establish new ones in a place that was the subject of a peace agreement, but they may not do so in a place taken by force." Then [Ibn al-Qāsim] said: "In [towns] laid out by the Muslims, such as Fusṭāṭ and Baṣra, they have no right to do such things unless they have a pact, which is fully fulfilled." Another said: "In any place conquered by force, where [*dhimmīs*] are allowed to remain, they may not establish new *kanīsas*." Here ends the necessary item abridged from [the *Mudawwana*]. The case cited in the question concerns what Muslims laid out, and there is no difference of opinion over [new *kanīsas*] being forbidden, since the views of others [than Ibn al-Qāsim] only concern a place taken by force, in which they have specifically been allowed to remain. It is for this reason that commentators of the book [*sc.* the *Mudawwana*], such as Abū Muḥammad Ṣāliḥ, al-Ṣarṣarī, al-Yaznāsinī, al-Shawshāwī, al-Ṭanjī, and [Abū 'l-Ḥasan] al-Maghribī, as well as a number of Shāfiᶜīs, declared that lands are of three types:

1. A land of Islam, in which it is not permissible to establish new *kanīsas*. According to some [this ruling is] a matter of agreement (*ittifāq*), while for others it is consensus (*ijmā*ᶜ). The meaning of those who use the term "agreement" is "consensus".

2. A land that was the subject of a peace agreement, where they may establish a new [place of worship] in accordance with what is in the contract (*al-kitāb*), contrary to ᶜAbd al-Malik and those who agree with him, insofar as they are living alongside Muslims.

3. A land taken by force, which Ibn al-Qāsim classified as a "land of the Muslims". Others, if they had settled in it, classified it as a land of peace agreement. The clear statement of those others is as regards that force—if they had not settled in it, but it only had Muslims, and then afterwards *dhimmīs* came there—it would be agreeable [241] that they not to have any new production due to initial conditionship on that, and secondly justification of it. For after their initial permission to remain there, it had come under the jurisdiction of the Muslims, and this would be ground for the agreement [not to let them establish a new place of worship]. This is the required interpretation of Abū ᶜUbayd's explanation of Ibn ᶜAbbās's statement, as has already been stated.

Regarding [Mālik's] statement in the book "unless they have a matter that they handed over", Abū Ḥafṣ al-ᶜAṭṭār, a contemporary of al-Tūnisī, Ibn Muḥriz, and their like, said in his explanatory comments (*ta*ᶜ*līq*) on the *Mudawwana*: "That 'handing over' only occurs at the time of occupation, not afterwards—meaning in the case of taking by force. But as for a land of the Muslims, what is authentic is the type of settlement in it. For if it were not granted them at the time of conquest, or the time of residence, then they would have no right for newly establishing [a place of worship], even if permission were to be subsequently given to them to do so. Thus, when the Christians who had taken up residence in Tunis established a new church in their hostel, and people complained of that, they revealed the pact of their residence, and there was found in it [the statement]: 'They should not be hindered from building a house for their worship." Were delayed permission to be valid, the complaint against them would have been pointless, since it would have been possible to grant them permission there and then; something similar will [later] be given from the *Aḥkām* of Ibn Sahl.

Shaykh Abū 'l-Ḥasan al-Maghribī said: "The imam may only grant them that right if the benefit of so doing is greater than the disadvantage, meaning that were they [the *dhimmī*s] to know about construction, planting, and reorganization, and the Muslims were not skilled in such a matter, and do not attend to it, as in Khaybar; then this benefit triumphs in protection for the achievement of construction. Similarly, if their being permitted to remain [at the time of conquest], or to take up residence among the Muslims [at a later date], brings about weakness and incapacity in the 'people of war', as was the case when the Almoravids brought over [to the Maghrib from Andalusia] people with whom a pact had been made, into a land of hostility, and they sought building of their places of worship at that time. Ibn al-Ḥājj gave a *fatwā* permitting them to do so, giving precedence to the advantage of enfeebling enemies, and as if their taking up residence were to cause the obtaining of great wealth, which can be made use of to fight the enemy. This was what the ruler of Tunis did, since he never tired of fighting the enemy, and hence this advantage took precedence. On the supposition that, in the case cited in the question, an obligation was made at the time of their taking up residence, such would not have been permissible, if they presented no advantage that could take precedence over the disadvantage of their making a public display of their religious tenets, which necessarily breaches the *sharī*ᶜ*a*, and is a cause of shame to the Muslims. But God knows best [the truth of all that].

In the third [section on] *jihād* in the *al-Wāḍiḥa* of Ibn Ḥabīb[77] [it is stated]: "Ibn al-Mājishūn and Muṭarrif and Aṣbagh and others said: 'No *kanīsa* is to be built in a territory of Islam, or in its protected area (*ḥarīm*), or in its surrounding district (ᶜ*amal*), even if [the *dhimmī*s] are isolated from the Muslims. The same applies to the people of a territory taken by force. When *jizya* is imposed on them, no *kanīsa* of theirs shall be left to them, unless it is in wreckage. [242] Thereafter, they shall not establish a [new] *kanīsa*, even if they are isolated from the Muslims. As for people whose territory was the subject of a peace agreement, if they are isolated from the Muslims, they are not to be prevented from establishing a place of worship or restoring an old one, whether or not this was laid down as a condition [in the peace agreement]. If they are living among the Muslims, they are forbidden to establish a place of worship.

If they [the Muslims] laid this down as a condition, it is not satisfactory to them. They are forbidden to restore pre-existing *kanīsas*, unless they stipulated it in their peace agreement, in which they are fully dealt with. But they are forbidden from making additions to it, either secretly or ostensibly". [Quotation ended]

Shaykh Abū Muḥammad [ᶜAbd Allāh] b. Abī Zayd al-Qayrawānī conveyed this view in his *Nawādir*,[78] confining to it, as the [Mālikī] *madh'hab* was under him; similarly. Ibn al-Munāṣif in [his] *Kitāb al-anjād.*[79] This statement clearly indicates a ban on establishing something new in the case cited, since it stipulates demolition in the territory of Islam, and the demolition of what is already in existence in a land taken by force, coupled with prohibiting a new creation. Making it compulsory to demolish pre-existing [places of worship] in the land taken by force makes it even more necessary to destroy newly built ones in the territory of Islam. However, he [al-Qayrawānī] held the view that the ban on establishing new ones necessitated there being none in existence. But to state that one demolishes what is not there is without meaning, contrary to what was already standing during conquest, for the supposition must be that such [a building] existed and hence it was necccesary to talk of its demolition. This is why nothing was said about demolition in *al-Mudawwana*,[80] where the author confined himself to talking of the prohibition on establishing new ones.

In the chapter on "Authority" (*al-sulṭān*) in the *Mustakhraja* of al-ᶜUtbī[81] [there is the following statement]: "Mālik was asked concerning *kanīsas* in al-Fusṭāṭ that had been newly established in districts (*khiṭaṭ*) of Islam: if they [the *Muslims*] had given them plots of land, or they [the *dhimmīs*] had rented them from the Muslims, building *kanīsas* on them". Mālik said: "My view is that this situation should be changed and [the *kanīsas*] should be demolished. Such should not be left abandoned, and there is no good in it." Ibn Rushd, commenting on this statement, said: "This is similar to what is in *al-Mudawwana* and other books, and I know of no difference of opinion over their demolition." The principle behind that is the statement related on the authority of [the Prophet], may God bless him and grant him peace, [who said]: "Let no Jewish or Christian one [referring to churches and synagogues] be raised among you." Then he cited the passage of *al-Wāḍiḥa*, and the difference of opinion between Ibn al-Qāsim and others over land taken by force. So, see the response of Mālik here, concerning *kanīsas* newly established in what was laid out by the Muslims, which is the meaning of [the phrase] "districts of Islam", which is the matter of the question without doubt, because of its ordinance in al-Fusṭāṭ.

In the *Mudawwana*, it was made clear that the matter concerns "what the Muslims have laid out", because he said: "the ones newly established in the districts of Islam." Hence are excluded areas under al-Fusṭāṭ's control,[82] which were taken by force, or were the subject of a peace agreement. So the area of agreement enunciated by Ibn Rushd, which is what the Muslims laid out, remains. [243] The statement of Ibn Rushd: "This area where there is an unambiguous statement regarding demolition", such as is in *al-Mudawwana* and other books—by which he meant [principally] the *Wāḍiḥa*—is proof of the soundness of what we indicated, following the statement of Ibn Ḥabīb on the evidence for demolition, inasmuch as it was not stated explicitly in the *Wāḍiḥa* and in *al-Mudawwana*. In his statement on the question: "if they [the *Muslims*] had given them plots of land, or they [the *dhimmīs*] had rented them from the Muslims, building *kanīsas* on them", he asked about any ruling when they owned control of a place; and that is what was meant by his statement: "they gave them the plots"; or if they owned its facility, which was what was meant by "they rented them from them and built a *kanīsa* on each of them".[83] Ownership by the one given a gift can only exist if the gift was not for building a *kanīsa*, since if it had been for that purpose it would have been repudiated, as it would amount to a Muslim setting up a pious benefaction for a *kanīsa*. Such a thing is to be repudiated, according to what the author of *al-Istighnā'*, and others, stipulated. The same goes for leasing. Ownership of a public establishment can only be made binding if it is not on the condition of building a *kanīsa*, since, if it were for such a purpose, [the contract] would have to be rescinded, according to what is in *al-Mudawwana* and other works. When the terms "outright gift" or "unlimited lease" were only aimed at the permissible form (*wajh*), Mālik took up the question on that, and only gave a ruling on demolition of the *kanīsa*. The matter remains valid with regard to other disposals. If the gift or lease were in a format that does not require possession of control or profit, then the answer would be the necessity of annulment, and the return of that to its owners, so they order them refutation of that; so in the meaning of a gift necessitating ownership, a valid sale necessitates ownership, so with him [Mālik] it is not allowable to build a *kanīsa* in the territory of Islam, since there is no difference between owning control through a gift and owning it through purchase. His statement in the question "if they gave them the vacant lots" means "or they bought them from them". What is meant is that the permissible form makes ownership obligatory.

The reason for the ban in all [these cases] is simply to highlight the pre-eminence of the honor of Islam, so that no other thing is as manifest as that. This was indicated in the *ḥadīth* that Ibn Rushd advanced as an argument; that is the saying of him [Prophet Muḥammad], upon whom be the blessing and peace of God: "Let no Jewish or Christian one be raised among you.[84] Islam is superior and nothing is above it." If the sale of control was based on the condition of the structure, then Ibn Rushd stipulated in *al-Jāmi*ᶜ that the ruling of Ibn al-Qāsim, and what he transmitted on Mālik's authority in *al-Mudawwana*, is cancellation, so the judgment is what we previously stated in regard to to giving about that.

It has been mentioned on the authority of Ibn Kināna that sale on such a condition is reprehensible (*makrūh*), and expires if such has occurred. In regard to this, a sale which takes place in a valid manner encompasses all rights of use, except for building a *kanīsa*, because of the right of Islam in it. [244] Hence they only spoke here about what concerns the price; whether it could be given out as charity, either partially, or not at all. They did not speak about what concerns the building and of a *kanīsa* and its demolition, some of them depending on the locality of talk about its specific nature, since this is a general [problem] if one considers the circumstances of every land which is adjudged to be a "territory of Islam". Nevertheless, al-Lakhmī referred to that at the end of what he said on the question of selling a building to be used as a *kanīsa*. He said: "I do not consider that the price of the building should be denied to [the seller]", meaning when the sale takes place "since permission of the activity of a *kanīsa* is not up to the seller, for if they had been given it and they were made an obligation over it, then they would refrain [from so doing]." You see how he made a ruling relating to the *kanīsa* in this particular form; i.e. a ruling about *kanīsa*s in general.

Since the meaning of the problem [raised] in *al-ᶜUtbiyya* is as we have stated, he did not say in the question "provided that they build". He merely said: "They build the *kanīsa*s on it", i.e. they build *kanīsa*s after giving or leasing [has occurred]. If it had been the "response" (*jawāb*) to a conditional phrase (*sharṭ*), he would have made it jussive without a *nūn*." The existence of the *nūn* is evidence of the truth of what we have stated, for even though Ibn Mālik and a [certain] group [of grammarians] allowed the use of the jussive in the response to a conditional phrase in the perfect indicative, others declared it unallowable, except in the case of [the verb] *kāna*, except in the imperative, when it is necessary." This is the correct [view], since such a usage is not selected by the Qurᵓān or in classical usage (*faṣīḥ al-kalām*) except with a *jazm*. Whoever allows use of the indicative [in the response to a past condition], considers it preponderate, and what falls within such a category is not to be used. The crux of the matter is that the ruling in regard to the *kanīsa*, whether the subject of a stipulation or not, is equal, as we have previously stated on the authority of al-Lakhmī.[85] God it is who guides aright.

When al-Tūnisī talked of the problem of establishing new *kanīsa*s, he cited and depended on what is in *al-Mudawwana*. He considered Ibn al-Qāsim's position on territories conquered by force to be correct, rather than the position taken by the others. There is no disagreement, according to him, about [the position regarding] what the Muslims lay out. As for Ibn Yūnus, after citing what is in the *Mudawwana*, he cited what is in *al-Wāḍiḥa*, limitizing himself to both. Both discussions are unambiguous about the ban on establishing new *kanīsa*s in the matter in the question. The two books necessarily agree upon that, and it is the correct [view] as Ibn Rushd declared. As for al-Lakhmī, he stated as follows: "There is a difference of opinion about *kanīsa*s in the territories of the Muslims, in regard to those taken by force, where the inhabitants were allowed to remain, and those areas laid out by the Muslims in which *dhimmī*s dwelt along side of them. There are three views:

(i) Ibn al-Qāsim stated: "[*Dhimmī*s] may not establish a new *kanīsa* in any part of the territories of Muslim lands, taken by force and where they settled, or what was laid out by the Muslims, where *dhimmī*s dwelt in it with them, unless they had been granted it, and it was fully given to them.

(ii) Others said: "They may establish new ones in a territory taken by force, if they settled in it. The obvious inference of the statements of the two of them is that a pre-existing [structure] in it could be left.

(iii) Ibn al-Mājishūn said [as reported] in the book of Ibn Ḥabīb: "As for the inhabitants of a territory taken by force, when *jizya* is imposed, no *kanīsa* of theirs shall be left to them, [245] except destructed. [245] Thereafter, they shall not establish a new *kanīsa*, even if they are isolated from the lands of Islam. As for the people whose territory was the subject of a peace agreement, they shall not establish a new *kanīsa* in the territories of the Muslims. If that was made a condition for them, it would not be allowed. They are forbidden to restore their pre-existing *kanīsas* if they fall into disrepair, unless this was stipulated for them in that [peace agreement], in which case it is to be fully given to them. They are forbidden to make any addition to it, either perceptible or intrinsic. If they are isolated from the lands of Islam and there are no Muslims living among them, they may establish new *kanīsas*." His statement is ended, and it has the meaning of what is in *al-Mudawwana* and *al-Wāḍiḥa*, with no added, or reduced, material. Whoever contemplates it, will know from it the agreement on forbidding new construction in areas laid out by Muslims, which is the matter of the question from him.

Summary of the views of the Jurisprudents on Kanīsas in the Territories of Islam

Ibn ᶜArafa[86] abridged the statement of al-Lakhmī in a way that presumes absolute disagreement over [the issue of] establishing new *kanīsas*, even in what Muslims had laid out, if [the *dhimmīs*] had not been granted that. Such is not to be found in what al-Lakhmī said in any form. All those who in later times cited the statement of al-Lakhmī cited it correctly, making no mention of such disagreement, if [the *dhimmīs*] had not been granted that, except in the case of territory taken by force. What al-Lakhmī meant to do by his statement "there is a difference of opinion about *kanīsas*", was to mention difference of opinion in a general fashion, for sometimes, in areas laid out by the Muslims, they will not be granted that [right to establish *kanīsas*] and sometimes they will. In a land taken by force there would sometimes be pre-existing *kanīsas*, and sometimes there would not be, and in each case they will sometimes be granted [the right] to establish new ones, and sometimes not. His statement is inclusive of all that, since this is his interpretation of *al-Mudawwana*. According to him, the topic of discussion is an examination of continuing existence of the old [*kanīsas*], in consolidation if they are given [such a thing]. Hence he expressed himself with the words "there have been differences of opinion about *kanīsas*", and not speaking of creating new ones. He mentioned three views of all of these [matters] which are taken from *al-Mudawwana* and *al-Wāḍiḥa*. They are as follows:

1. The view of Ibn al-Qāsim that pre-existing ones in territories taken by force should be allowed to remain, and that new ones should be forbidden in such lands, as well as in areas laid out by the Muslims, unless a gift was granted.

2. The view of other than him, which is similar to his, except that it does not make the condition of a gift [that could be granted] to create new *kanīsas* in lands taken by force.

3. The view of ᶜAbd al-Mālik that pre-existing ones should absolutely be demolished and no new ones established, in both areas set up by Muslims and territory taken by force [246] under any circumstances, whether or not they were given it.

An understanding of these views from the statement of al-Lakhmī only becomes clear after reflection, inasmuch as he made his phrase "if that is stipulated to them, it should not be granted" to refer back to the two problems which preceded it—to wit: territory taken by force, and that which is subject to a peace agreement in which Muslims dwell. Now if [an agreement about] territory subject to a peace agreement is not to be honored, how much less would it be honored in the case of territory taken by force. If you reflect on these views, you will realise that there is agreement over prohibiting the establishment of new [*kanīsas*] in areas laid out [by the Muslims], if they have not been granted [a specific privilege]. When Ibn ᶜArafa expressed that, through his phrase "there were differences of opinion over the establishment of new *kanīsas*", al-Lakhmi did not turn to it, and so it was necessary for him to pursue its contradiction with the expression of al-Lakhmī and its lack of his agreement over its transmission. Al-Lakhmī's report of disagreement, in the form in which we have given it, is correct, since it is thus, according to the imams of the [Mālikī] *madh'hab*, following what they understood from *al-Mudawwana* and *al-Wāḍiḥa*. Nevertheless, many of them made no distinction between pre-existing [*kanīsa*s] and others in the territory taken by force, as we shall later indicate. And this is the inevitable conclusion to be drawn from what was earlier cited on the authority of ᶜUmar b. ᶜAbd al-ᶜAzīz and others. It should not be suggested that Ibn ᶜArafa came across something which is not in al-Lakhmī, for we would say that, since Ibn ᶜArafa traced his citation to the citation of al-Lakhmī, such a claim must fall. God it is who gives success.

Consensus of the Advice Council of Cordova on the Prohibition of Establishing New Kanīsas in the Territories of Islam

In the *Nawāzil* of Ibn Sahl,[87] after some matters, the sources of which were from the *Aḥkām* of Ibn Ziyād [we read] that a man attacked some *dhimmī*s in a synagogue (*shunūgha*) of theirs, which he had determined to have been newly established. The Advice Council (*ahl al-shūrā*) of Cordova was asked about that, and they gave the following reply: "We understand—may God grant you success—the existing testimonies (*shihādāt*) to mean that the synagogue was a newly established one, and we have seen testimonies that make it obligatory to demolish it, after giving a warning to its people. In the laws of Islam there cannot be newly established by *dhimmī*s—Jews or Christians—either synagogues or churches in the towns of Islam, or amongst Muslims. Delivered by ᶜUbayd Allāh b. Yaḥyā, Muḥammad b. Lubāba, Ibn Ghālib, Ibn Walīd, Saᶜd b. Muᶜādh, Yaḥyā b. ᶜAbd al-ᶜAzīz, Ayyūb b. Sulaymān and Saᶜīd b. Jubayr". These imams are men to be relied on in the giving of advice in Cordova. They were in agreement, and no one opposed them over the question of demolishing newly established *kanīsa*s in the towns of Islam, and that is certainly what the case cited in the question deals with. Their statement necessitates that this ruling is one on which there is consensus, since their phrase "there is not in the laws of Islam any new establishment" means "there is not in the law-schools [247] of Islam any [allowance for] newly establishing [*kanīsa*s]", since the law-schools are what have been set up for [determining] the laws. Its being a matter of consensus is correct, and the clarification of it will come. In their phrase "in the towns of Islam" is an indication of the emergence of suitability if they are alone in it, since the ruling about them is not like that, according to what has been said.

After Ibn Sahl had mentioned their formal legal opinion, he gave it up and took the statement of *al-Mudawwana* and *al-Wāḍiḥa* as proof of the correctness [of demolishing such synagogues], pointing out that they had merely relied on the two aforementioned books as their authority. After finishing with this problem, Ibn Sahl followed it with another problem, from which may be understood how well he indicates things to people who are perceptive. In the *Kāfī* of Abū ᶜUmar b. ᶜAbd al-Bārr[88] is the following statement:

> People whose territory was conquered by force may not establish any new *kanīsa*, they having the status of *dhimmī*s; and *dhimmī*s do not have the right to establish in the territory of Islam a new *kanīsa* which they had not [previously] had in the land of Islam. As for *kanīsa*s of theirs, which were the subject of a pact and a peace agreement, they are not be deprived of them, nor shall they be changed to their disadvantage. As for the towns which the Muslims laid out and which the *dhimmī*s dwelt in alongside them, it is not permissible for them to establish a new *kanīsa* therein. It has been said that if they were dwelling alongside the Muslims in a place of theirs in which there was a *kanīsa*, and they [later] relocated together with the Muslims and assisted them, then they would have the same rights [in the new location] and should not be prevented from having a single *kanīsa*, unless that were a condition imposed upon them. End of verbatim quotation.

He was explicit about banning new establishment in areas laid out by the Muslims. It is apparent that this is something agreed upon, since he did not mention disagreement in a specific fashion. This has to do with *dhimmīs* having a *kanīsa*, being together with the Muslims, and then relocating together with them, and laying out a new area for settlement. This is not what the case cited in the question is about, since the place in question is one which the Muslims laid out by themselves. In the *Jawāhir* of Ibn Shās[89] is the statement: "If they"—that is the *dhimmīs* —"are in a town built by the Muslims they shall not be given the possibility of building a *kanīsa*. Similarly, if we obtain by conquest the perpetual lease of a town of theirs, the imam may not confirm the existence of a *kanīsa* in it. On the contrary, it is obligatory to tear down their *kanīsas* which are in it. You see how he was quite explicit about their not being given the possibility of building a *kanīsa* in a town built by the Muslims. This squarely addresses the case cited in the question.

In the *Dhakhīra* of al-Qarāfī[90] is the following text: "The Seventh Inquiry concerning what they, i.e. the *dhimmīs*, must do, in conformity with contraction of the *jizya*". It falls into three categories:

1. *Kanīsas*. They are not to be given the possibility of constructing them in a town built by the Muslims, or which the Muslims took by force. [Pre-existing] *Kanīsas* must be torn down. In the ᶜ*Umda* of Ibn ᶜAskar al-Baghdādī,[91] a celebrated Mālikī, whom Khalīl[92] quoted in a number of places in the *Tawḍīḥ*, is the following statement: "They are not to be given the possibility of establishing a *kanīsa* in the Abode of Islam. [248] The *kanīsas* in territories of theirs taken by force are to be torn down." Commenting on this, he said:

> If their territory is conquered by force, it is obligatory to demolish any synagogue, church or monastery, as if the territory had assumed the legal status of the Abode of Islam. If [*dhimmīs*] traveled from their territory to the Abode of Islam they would not be given the possibility of establishing anything of that nature.

This last statement is the essence of the case in question, since [the Jews of Touat] moved into a location (*dār*) in which only Muslims were living, and he stated explicitly that [in such a case] they should not be given the possibility of establishing anything of that nature. The obvious matter is: had they had a *kanīsa* in the place from which they moved, then how would it be if they had not had one? Whoever reflects on the statements of Ibn Shās, al-Qarāfī, and Ibn ᶜAskar will realize that they are in opposition to al-Lakhmī's reference to *al-Mudawwana*, for according to them there is no difference in a territory taken by force between a pre-existing [*kanīsa*]—according to what has preceded—and a new one.

In sum, the scholars—may God be pleased with them—have pronounced on the problem in earlier times and recently, and have nothing more to say beyond what we have presented—even the commentators on the *Risāla* such as al-Zanātī and Ibn ᶜUmar etc., who do not go beyond what we have said. The last scholar who pronounced on the matter was the *qāḍī* al-ᶜUqbānī in his book *Tuḥfat al-nāẓir fi taghyīr al-manākir*,[93] where he included statements by earlier and later scholars, none of which falls outside the scope of what we have mentioned. In this work he mentioned that *Shaykh* Abū 'l-Faḍl Qāsim b. Saᶜīd al-ᶜUqbānī was asked whether the Jews of Touat had had removed [from them] the hospitality and nourishments that ᶜUmar had decreed. Mālik came out with their removal from *dhimmīs*, because they were not to be fully donated [by Muslims]. So he said that what are obligatory for the Jews of Touat are *jizya*, hospitality, and nourishments, since they had escaped the limit of humiliation due to them, and terrible punishment on the Day of Gathering and Requital did not prevent them from such a thing.[94] "And those who have ill treated shall know what hereafter transforms them [on the Day of Judgement]". [Qurʾān, 26:227]

He went on to say: "What the Jews do nowadays, while on travel, such as riding horses, using expensive saddles, wearing boastful clothing, and the embellishment of Muslims, in wearing spurred boots and turbans, is a foul abomination and a shocking disclaim. All possible steps should be taken to bring this to an end. They may make some legal justification for that, alleging that they fear for their persons and property, if is seen upon them the clothing by which they are known. In this matter they are liars, since we have witnessed that they enjoy strong security among the Arabs, and great good fortune, because of the benefit that people hope to derive from them. An Arab will allow himself and his whole family to be exterminated to save the Jew who is with him. [249] All that remains is that when they found comfort among the uncouth and despotic [nomadic] Arabs who did not contest them, they dressed in the most luxurious Muslim clothes, since they did not do that in the settled areas. May God quell their pomp, and give strength to Islam through their abasement and humility. Nowadays they are into greater matters than that. May God restore the split in Islam,[95] for the hearts of rulers are in His hands.

The Fatwā of al-ᶜAbdūsī on harshness in the ban of establishing of a shrine for Jews

May God have mercy on the *shaykh*, the Imam, the protector of the Maghrib, Abū 'l-Qāsim al-ᶜAbdūsī, a resident of Tunis. He gave a *fatwā* on the matter of the meaning of the question of what restores appearance through the brighness and light that is upon it. This is the text of the question: Praise be to God. My master, may God be pleased with you all, and grant Muslims enjoyment of your life; [please give] your reply concerning a newly built village in the territory of the Muslims, where Jews—may God degrade them—set up a new *kanīsa*, and they undertook worship in it, in accordance with their polytheism, to the point that God inspired some eminent Muslims of the people of knowledge and religion, who wished God's blessing through it; so he saw of the breach in religion, and the disgrace upon Muslims, that elements of idolatry were installed in the lands of the Muslims, and so he ordered that the aforementioned *kanīsa* be destroyed and its influence obliterated, and thus something greatly objectionable was cut off and heresy extinguished. Then the aforementioned Jews—may God humiliate them—wished to renew the construction of it and to return to what was they were up to in promoting their religion and surviving their practice. Through that no protection for them was concluded, nor was any *jizya* imposed upon them. Can they deal with that, or not? Your reply, you rewarded ones, and peace [be upon you].

The Reply: Praise be to God. They may neither establish, nor restore, any [place of worship] in the territories of the Muslims. So said Ibn al-Qāsim on the authority of Mālik, in the section on "Pay and protection" (*Kitāb al-jaᶜl wa 'l-ijāra*) in *al-Mudawwana*.[96] If they do this, after having been forbidden to do so, it constitutes a breaking of the [bond of] protection that they have. There is a consensus to the effect that none of them may establish a new place of worship or restore [an old one] in the territories of the Muslims. If they are forbidden to do so and do not desist, this constitutes an act of breaking the pact. As a result, their wealth goes to the Muslims, and their offspring are deemed liable to the dominion of militarians in the non-Muslim lands. And their children and women-folk belong to the Muslims.

The *shaykhs* of the Maghrib gave *fatwās* before this, saying that they had no bond [of protection] without this, so what is your thought on this matter? Whoever gives a reason for restoring the synagogue to them, and supports them with that, or causes them to be successful, believing in its embellishment, then he is an unbeliever, or, if not, then at least a sinner upon whom descends the curse of God and His Messenger—may God bless him and grant him peace—[250] for he said: "Whoever commits a misdeed, or gives shelter to one who commits a misdeed, upon him be the curse of God and His angels and the whole of humanity". He also said: "Whoever was pleased with what people did, was a sharer with them". Our Lord—Exalted is His Majesty—said: "Thou wilt not find folk who believe in God and the Last Day loving those who oppose God and His Messenger, even though they be their fathers [or their sons or their brethren or their clan. As for such people, He has written faith upon their hearts and strengthened them with a Spirit from Him. And He enters them into gardens with rivers beneath them, wherein they will continually exist—God being pleased with them, and they with Him. They are God's party. Lo! is it not God's party who are successful?" [Qurʾān 58:22].[97] And change fears him at the end. The traditions and *ḥadīths* on this subject are more numerous than given here'.

Abū 'l-Qāsim al-ᶜAbdūsī—may God treat him gracefully—wrote: "Take a look at the reply of this imam—may God be pleased with him—as if it were manifested that that did not occur from them, except through designated Muslims, who apply it as a pretext to attain their desire. Whilst his command on that is under way between unbelief and sinfulness, necessitating the curse of God, the angels, and the whole of humanity, and fear of changing of the conclusion, we seek protection of God from what forces us to go astray. Don't you see that he did not mention this section to him in the inquiry, nor was it hinted to him in it?

But when God granted him some light of insight, it was revealed that he would not be that except through that.

If, in the *madh'hab*, there had been no text, except what occurred in the reply of this *shaykh*, it would be convincing in the issue of the question of how about that, with the texts of former and recent persons?[98]

Maghribī shaykhs in the Age of the Marīnids (1196-1299) gave fatwās denying Protection for Jews

What he referred to in the reply was that the *shaykh*s of the Maghrib had no protection for themselves in what was below/before this; that is their selling wine to Muslims, and their conspiracy in doing this after being banned from so doing. This was agreed upon in the days of Yūsuf b. Ya^cqūb b. ^cAbd al-Ḥaqq al-Marīnī,[99] so they were killed for that and made prisoners throughout all the Marīnid territory, as was mentioned by al-Khazrajī, the *qāḍī* of Bādis and elsewhere in Al-Rīf[100] in the reign of Yūsuf b. Ya^cqūb. What we have obtained about Mālikī imams on this question is not what only they have done. Indeed, that is the ruling of the people of all schools of law (*madhāhib*). This Shāfi^cī imam says: "It is necessary for the imam, in relation to the *dhimmīs,* to make limits on all that he gives them, and to take it from them, so that they raise up the *jizya* and submit it, being humble, provided that the rulings of Muslims act upon them when a claimant makes a demand of them, and provided that, in any metropolis of the Muslims, they do not initiate any *kanīsa* and do not assemble for their worship—[etc.], to the end of what he mentioned: "We deducted from him the needed place". That was quoted of by Ibn al-Munāṣif and Ibn al-Mundhir. Al-Māwardī and al-Ghazālī said something like that, in dealing with what is relevant to the matter of the demand. [251] *Shaykh* Abū 'l-Ḥasan al-Qaddūri of the Ḥanafī *madh'hab* said in his *Mukhtaṣar*: "It is not permissible to initiate a church (*bī^ca*) or a synagogue (*kanīsa*) in the territory of Islam."[101]

When Ibn al-Mundhir quoted what we mentioned from al-Shāfi^cī, he quoted something like it from doctrinaires—that is Ḥanafites. And he mentioned that Aḥmad ibn Ḥanbal—may God be pleased with him—said: "*Dhimmī*s may not demonstrate of their religion any matter that was not in their peace agreement. This is what Ibn Ḥazm al-Ẓāhirī mentioned in the book *Marātib al-Ijmā*ᶜ: "He has agreement of the scholars (*al-ᶜulamā*ᵓ) on the taking of *jizya* from Scripturists (*ahl al-Kitāb*), provided they do not initiate a synagogue or a church." These scholars of Islam—Mālikīs, Shāfiᶜīs, Ḥanafīs, Ḥanbalīs, and Ẓāhirīs,[102]—have nothing [in their law opinions] except prevention of initiating *kanīsas*.

[It results from all this that] the problem is one on which there is consensus. We have already mentioned that some of the commentators on *al-Mudawwana* declared the transmission of a consensus on this matter. We indicated, immediately following the statement of Ibn Sahl to the necessary *fatwā* of the imams of consultancy (*a*ᵓ*immat al-shūrā*) in Cordova, that the problem was one on which there was consensus. Abū Bakr al-Ṭurṭūshī also declared there was consensus on it, as did Ibn Badrān and Ibn Ḥazm, in addition to al-ᶜAbdūsī in his preceding *fatwā*. The answer is for every capable Muslim to endeavor demolition of the synagogue for which he is responsible with the power of his capacity. He should make as much effort as possible to do that, since this is one of the greatest jihads. If anyone should try to stop him from doing that, then the response of the Imam of the Maghrib, Abū 'l-Qāsim al-ᶜAbdūsī is complete regarding him, inasmuch as he assigned him as intermediating between "unbelief" and "sinfulness" which calls forth upon him the curse of God, His angels, and all human beings.

Continued Existence of what is objected to, or its Abundance, does not change the Legal Ruling on it.

There is no argument for them on prolonged possession [of the land on which the synagogue is built], since its objective is to show control of the possession; and it has already been stated that, in consideration of the rights of Islam, ownership of the perpetual lease, whether by valid gift or sale, does not permit them to build a synagogue.

So what about possession that falls short of outright ownership? The authoritative texts of the [Mālikī] *madh'hab* are in agreement that what has in it the right of God Most High has no effect for possession, like property the yield of which is devoted to pious purposes. Rather, they stated that authority over them is not suspended, even if a judge issues a judgment concerning them. How is it, with no judgment about it, just as no proof of theirs on the existence of that, frequently in large urbanities, since continued existence of what is objected to, or its abundance, does not change the legal ruling on it? Since there is no objection greater than abandon of worship, necessitating killing for disbelief, or transgression, of a restriction [of God], many people, both strangers and highly bred, have continued in this. That has not changed legal ruling on it, since scholars ceased not, in ancient and modern times, to specify the necessity of killing such a person, whether an unbeliever or a transgressor of [divine] restriction, and there is no consideration with them on its multiple existence. Similarly, they did not cease specifying prohibition concerning the matter of the question, [252] and on destruction [of a synagogue] after its being built. They have no consideration either on the practice being widespread, or its having endured for long. No one disapproves of texts that necessitate such action and rejects their slaughter, except someone who denies the validity of the *sharīᶜa*, striving to destroy it. May God preserve us from abandoning or renouncing the religion of him who was sent [by God], of the best family through Maᶜadd b. ᶜAdnān, a master of Prophets and Messengers [of God],[103] and clarifier of methods and paths, who was sent with guidance and the religion of Truth, that it might triumph over all other religion, "however much the disbelievers are averse." [Qurʾān, 9:33] And he was ordered to combat those who believe not in God or the Last Day,[104] nor do they forbid what God and His Messenger have forbidden; nor do they profess the Religion of Truth until they pay *jizya* by force—being lowly.[105] And may God bless our master Muḥammad, and his family and Companions, as long as the world exists, and the word of God is supreme, and may He grant him [Muḥammad], and all of them, peace. Praise be to God, the Lord of the Worlds. Its issue[106] is determined in the writing of the jurisprudent, the pious and sincerely advisory imam, Abū ᶜAbd Allāh Sīdī Muḥammad b. Yūsuf al-Sanūsī,[107] in the following text:

> Praise be to God, the Lord of the Worlds, and blessing and peace be upon our Master Muḥammad, the Seal of the Prophets and Master of the Messengers. And from His Faith comes liberal religious law (*sharīᶜa*), lasting and dominant over all faiths, until the Day of Judgment.

From the humble servant of God Almighty, Muḥammad b. Yūsuf al-Sanūsī—may God Almighty forgive him and his parents with no distress—to the brother in God, the beloved in the personality of God Most High, the advocater of what is obliterated in foul time of the religious duty of the affair with recognition, and denial of the atrocity—the practice of which, especially nowadays, is knowledge of the broadening in intellectual masculinity and Islamic zeal and flourishing of the spirit, through the Noble of Faith, the master Abū ᶜAbd Allāh Muḥammad b. ᶜAbd al-Karīm al-Maghīlī—may God conserve his life, and put blessing upon his religious creed and his worldly existence, and make an end for us, for him, and for all other Muslims, with happiness and pardon, with no suffering, the day when we meet Him.

After Peace upon you and Mercy and Blessing, there reached us, sir, faith fervor, and intellectual valor imputed on you of the changing of initiation by Jews—may God Most Exalted humiliate them and supress their disbelief—of a *kanīsa* in settlements of Muslims; and that you incited the people of Tamantit to destroy the *kanīsa*s owned by Jews in their territories. So they made a halt on the one hand, to the sectarians who opposed you on that. And, on account of that, you sent to our town questions and documents in which they stimulate the ambitions of learned folk to see in the question the view of people of justice and honesty; and they declared in them an unequivocal and convincing declaration to every delirium and starvation that declines people of affection and inclination.

So be aware, O my brother, [253] that I never saw who would succeed in responses to this resolution, and offer his capability in fulfillment of the truth, and the ardent desire of 'Believers' (*ahl al-īmān*) on this question would be gratified; and it would not take reversal, due to the strength of his faith and the clear evidence of his ascertainty in regard to what demonic prejudice points out from the hypocrisy of some whose vehemence causes wariness, and fears that compulsion or diminution in status will fall upon him—other than the *Shaykh* and Imam, the model of distinguished persons, the observer and investigator, Abū ᶜAbd Allāh Muḥammad b. ᶜAbd al-Jalīl al-Tanasī[108]—may God the Highly Exalted bless him and grant him and Muslims his continued existence—and support him with long hygiene and good health; increasing his life in this world, and the other world in his sublimity and advancement. For he—may God award him goodness—expanded elucidation of the Truth, and its characteristics opened the mind, and verified transmission and comprehension. So he persisted in that, until he revealed from the light of his faith, the exterminator of the glooms of infidelity, with his influences being the greatest adoption. According to what you take interest in, regarding his written response, this is at the end of it. So may the people of Tamantit and other Muslim folk depend on what he revealed of the truth in that response. And may they reject what opposed him, if they wish for triumph through the dignity of Islam and its esteem, and attainment of the goal of what is correct. And God the Glorified is the one responsible to grant us, and all other Muslims, devotedness to the Truth, suppression of the false, and evaluation of the religion of Islam, and to eliminate paganism and its effects from all lands of Muḥammad—may God bless him and grant him peace.

Peace be upon you—and on whoever focuses on this document—and the Mercy of God and His Blessings.

CHAPTER FIVE

Degradation and Diaspora of the Tamantit Jews

After al-Maghīlī received and studied the *fatwā* of al-Tanasī, he was convinced of support for his attitude against Jews, and gathered together enough supporters to help him destroy the synagogue and sabotage the Jewish community. Many Jews of Tamantit were killed, especially trying to defend their synagogue, while others fled, and eventually settled in other northern Saharan oases.

His attitude is explained by the biographer Ibn ᶜAskar as follows:

> He held the view that the Jews—may God curse them—had no [bond of] protection (*dhimma*) on account of their having broken it by their association with the men of authority among the Muslims, [an action] which negated the humiliation and abasement, stipulated in the payment of *jizya*, and that the breaking [of this pact] by some of them redounded upon all of them. He revoked the inviolability of their lives and property, and ruled that dealing with them was more important than dealing with any other "unbelievers".[109]

However, exactly how al-Maghīlī persuaded Tamantit Muslims to degrade or dismiss the Jewish community of their village, and to destroy the Jews' house of worship, is not clear; especially since we know that the Jews had often collaborated with the Muslims in trans-Saharan trade. He would no doubt have used the *fatwā* of al-Tanasī to show them that the very existence of the Tamantit synagogue was Islamically "illegal". He may also have argued that the participation of Jews in Saharan trading would come eventually to affect the Muslims and impoverish them.[110] The economic "threat" of Jews may well have been an issue that al-Maghīlī personally thought of, as other Muslims of Tlemcen may also have done; and he offered seven *mithqāls* for anyone who killed a Jew (for him).[111]

The number of Jews in North Africa was increasing as they immigrated from Andalusia, and many came with considerable trading experience. Not only were such communities increasing and settling in Muslim-occupied locations, but there were other threats to the gold trade from West Africa, particularly from the Portuguese. The Portuguese began to occupy ports on the western coastal areas of Africa, beginning in the Maghrib in 1415 with Ceuta, just opposite the Iberian penninsula, and by 1471 they had reached the area later known as the Gold Coast, setting up a location fairly close to a gold mine of the Akan forests,[112] from where gold was taken to Jenne, and then to Timbuktu, where North African traders could obtain it; also, on the coast of what is now Mauritania, at Arguin, Portuguese occupants strove to persuade caravans crossing the Sahara from Walata to stop at their location to trade them the gold that they were carrying. Gold bearers were also attracted to locations on the west coast of Morocco, where the Portuguese had set up their locations.[113] Hence, for North African Arabs (or Berbers), access to West African gold was declining by the late fifteenth century, though not specifically due to Jewish trade activity. But such a decline may well have made North Africans—especially those of Tlemcen—regret the immigration of Jews, who would, in some sense, share their economy. So, the troubled feeling that the Portuguese seizure of gold trade, plus an increase in immigrant Jewish populations, would have had on Muslim inhabitants of the Tlemcen and Touat areas, may well have influenced al-Maghīlī, and also al-Tanasī, to look for ways to diminish Jewish populations involved in trading avtivities—but using *sharīᶜa*-based arguments, rather than just economic issues. Arguments for the illegitimacy of a Jewish synagogue set up in a Muslim-occupied territory constituted the principal reasoning[114] behind Muslims' activity—destroying the synagogue and killing any Jews who tried to protect it—thus leading to total degradation of the Jewish community, either by its members dying, or fleeing out of Tamantit as an area of threatening violence.

Certainly, the Mālikī *sharīᶜa* condemned the creation of a worship-building by any *dhimmīs* within a territory controlled by Muslims, but no argument was made to prove that the Jews of Tamantit had set up a synagogue after Muslims had occupied—or set up—the oasis sector. In any case, if Jews had had a synagogue in Tamantit before Muslims occupied the area, then they would have had the right to retain it. In fact, no proof of the *sharīᶜa* obligation to destroy the synagogue ever clearly came about. The Jews of Tamantit no doubt sought to prevent such destruction, which may well be why some of them were killed and others saw it necessary to quit their home location. Muslims may also have convinced themselves of the *sharīᶜa* illegality of the Jews' adoption of clothing and riding animals similar to what Muslims used, as dealt with in al-Tanasī's *fatwā*. So persecution of the Jews may not necessarily have been based only on the existence of a synagogue.

Whether or not the life of al-Maghīlī was threatened by that violent action, he left Tamantit just after the destruction of the synagogue, traveling across the Sahara—initially to Kano, and then to Gao. In both places he was an advisor to the local ruler. He had already written a letter of advice to Sultan Muḥammad Rumfa of Kano, and while seeing him in the early 1490s wrote for him on the obligations of a Muslim ruler: *Tāj al-Dīn fī mā yajib ᶜalā 'l-mulūk.*[115] After about three years in Kano, al-Maghīlī moved on to Gao, the "capital" of the Songhay empire, ruled by Askiya *al-Ḥājj* Muḥammad (*reg.* 1493–1529).

That ruler asked him for replies to a series of six major questions about Islamic ruling, to which al-Maghīlī responded immediately with very full answers.[116] In addition to those "replies", al-Maghīlī also influenced the Askiya to forbid the entry of Jews into the territory of the Songhay empire. Leo Africanus also observed: "This king [of Timbuktu] is a declared enemy of Jews. He does not wish any to live in the town. If he hears it said that a Berber merchant frequents them, or does trade with them, his [the merchant's] goods are confiscated".[117] No Jews are known to have again visited Timbuktu until the nineteenth century, when some were re-engaged in trade there.[118] While in Gao, al-Maghīlī got news that his son, who had remained in Tamantit, had been killed there, allegedly by Jews. It is doubtful if the Jewish community alone was responsible, and the death was most probably part of an intra-communal feud, in which both Jews and Muslims were involved on both sides.

Askiya Muḥammad was apparently persuaded to arrest all the Touat men in Gao, but it is not clear that all of these were Jews, or even all from Tamantit. On the intercession of Maḥmūd b. ᶜUmar, the *qāḍī* of Timbuktu, they were released, since they clearly bore no guilt for the murder. However, Ibn ᶜAskar reports that Jews were not allowed to enter Songhay territory, and anyone found to be trading with a Jew could be despoiled. He claimed that this was a general rule, as a result of al-Maghīlī's teachings.[119] Thus, it was not the destruction of two important Saharan Jewish communities that alone led to the general impoverishment and social degradation of the Jews of the oases, but the success of an uncompromising campaign to force those *dhimmīs* to "observe humility in their words, deeds, and all aspects of their behavior, so they would be under the heel of every Muslim—man, woman, free, or slave."[120]

Al-Maghīlī may even have taken part in the pillaging and killing of Jews in the other nearby Saharan oasis of Gourara in 1492. Also, in 1518, the Jews of Tlemcen are said to have been "ransacked", leading them to later become beggars[121]—though not directly through al-Maghīlī, who had died in 1504.

CHAPTER SIX

Conclusion

The degradation of the Jewish community of Tamantit in the late fifteenth century was not the first—and not even the last—misfortune that Jews suffered. In the first century C.E. the Romans occupied the homeland of Jews in what is now Israel. With part of their "capital" of Jerusalem being destroyed by the Romans in 70 C.E., the Jews moved out of the area to north, south, east, and west. Some went down into the Arabian peninsula, even to what is now the Yemen, while others went to oasis-type settlements such as Yathrib, which became known as Medina (*Madīnat al-nabī*) when the Prophet Muḥammad migrated there from Mecca in 622. Many Jews were captured by the Romans, and then sold as slaves into areas of North Africa, much of which was soon after taken over by the Romans, and then the Byzantines. Many Jews had first moved into North Africa after the destruction of their temple in Jerusalem by Nebuchadnezzar in 586 B.C.E.

The degradation of the Tamantit Jewish community occurred in, or around, 1490, and some two years later there was anti-Jewish activity—set up by "a preacher of Tlemcen", perhaps al-Maghīlī—at the oasis of Gourara just north of Touat. The Andalusian-Moroccan explorer Leo Africanus (originally named al-Ḥasan b. Muḥammad al-Wazzān al-Zayyātī) relates:

> In Gourara there were some very rich Jews. The intervention of a preacher of Tlemcen set up the pillage of their goods, and most of them have been killed by the population. This event took place in the year when the Jews had been expelled from Spain and Sicily by the Catholic king.[122]

As for Tlemcen, Leo Africanus estimated the Jewish population as follows:

> There is a large quarter that contains some five hundred houses of Jews, nearly all rich, and wearing a yellow turban on their heads. These Jews have only been rich for a time, because on the death of [ruler] Abu Habdilla (Abū ᶜAbd Allāh Muḥammad V), they were "ransacked" in 923 H./1516–17 C.E., so much so that they are now almost beggars.[123]

We do not know in what way, or by whom, those Jews were "ransacked", but in the seventeenth century a French writer on Africa, Pierre Davity, said:

> Formerly, the Jews had ten large synagogues, which were not even sufficient for them; but after the death of the king Abu Abdala (Abū ᶜAbd Allāh [Muḥammad]), in the year of grace 1517, their number and their means were diminished. Nowadays they still hold the most beautiful road in Tlemcen.[124]

The Spanish Christians, who had made it desirable for Jews, as well as Muslims, to move out of Andalusia, and into North Africa down to 1492, began [themselves] to occupy coastal areas in what are now Algeria, Tunisia, and Libya, starting in 1509. Oran, on the Mediterranean coast just north of Tlemcen, was captured in 1509, and 4,000 people were killed, about 5,000 taken into captivity, and two mosques turned into churches. Jews also suffered there, and afterwards Jews of Bougie [Bajāya] and Tripoli were captured and taken into exile, while some took refuge in Italy and others moved into Egypt.[125] However, the Spaniards did not attempt to occupy interior areas of North Africa, but were, before long, dislodged from coastal cities by Ottoman sailors. Nevertheless, a Jewish writer states:

> Tlemcen was captured by the idolators in the year 5202 [1542 C.E.]... and about 1,500 Jews were killed or taken pris-

> oner. Some Jews went to Fez to ask the local community to ransom the captives, but they could not redeem all of them, because of their great number, and of prices that were higher than they were worth. Some of the people had fled prior to being taken, hoping to get away, and were subsequently caught, because the inhabitants of the place to which they had fled betrayed them to the idolaters.[126]

Whether the so-called "idolaters" were Spaniards is not clear, but it is possible that it is Spaniards being referred to—or, less likely, Ottomans, who are known to have occupied Tlemcen, though apparently not until 1555.

Despite the suppression of Jews in Tlemcen, a Jewish population survived into the twentieth century, when (in 1941) there were nearly five thousand Jews dwelling in that city.[127] However, after the establishment of the state of Israel in 1948—despite its conflicts with the Arab world—Jews from all parts of North Africa moved into the new Jewish nation.

Although Jews were banned from the Songhay empire—on the advice of al-Maghīlī—some evidently got there, and as Mungo Park explored western Africa in the late eighteenth century, he was told by an Arab he met near Walata that "there were many Jews at Tombuctoo, but they all spoke Arabic, and used the same prayers as the Moors".[128] In the nineteenth century more Jews came from North Africa (especially Morocco) to Timbuktu for commerce, and some documents of theirs—in Arabic, but many with a Hebrew remark at the beginning—still exist in Timbuktu, most accessible in the Centre de Documentation et de Recherches Historiques Ahmed Baba [CEDRAB], set up in 1973.[129] Morocco had become a refuge for Jews degraded in other areas of North Africa—including Tlemcen—or southwestern Europe. Hence, many Jews continued to survive, despite their evident unpopularity in what is now Algeria.[130] Although many Moroccan Jews moved to Israel after 1948, some still return to their Moroccan "home" on vacation every year, and are accepted in (and out again) without problems.

APPENDIX A

The Qur'ān on Jews

These quotations from the Qur'ān are based on Marmaduke Pickthall's translation (see Bibliography), with a few slight changes.

2:113 The Jews say that Christians follow nothing [true], and Christians say the same of the Jews; and they [all] pursue the Scripture. Thus say those who know not the like of what they say. So God will make judgment between them on the Day of Judgment, concerning what they differ on.

2:120 Neither Jews nor Christians will be pleased with you until you follow their creed. Say: "Surely the guidance of God is [true] guidance"; so if you follow their desires after what knowledge came to you, you will have from God no friend or helper.

3:67 Abraham was neither a Jew nor a Christian; but he was an upright man, who had surrendered [to Allah], and not of the idolaters.

5:18 Jews and Christians say: "We are sons of Allah and His beloved ones." Say: "Why then does He chastise you for your sins?" Rather, you are beings whom He created. He forgives whom He will, and chastises whom He will. Allah has sovereignty over the heavens and the earth and what lies between them; and to Him is the return journey.

5:51 O you who believe, take not Jews and Christians as friends. They are friends to one another. Whoso among you befriends them belongs to them. Surely, God does not guide the wrongdoers.

5:64 Jews say: "God's hand is fettered." Their hands are fettered, and they have been accursed for what they said. Rather, both His hands are widespread, and He bestows how He wills....

5:82 Thou wilt find the most hostile of people vis-à-vis those who believe [i.e. Muslims], to be the Jews and those who are idolaters. And thou wilt find the nearest of them in affection to those who believe to be those who say: "Lo! We are Christians."

9:30 The Jews say: "Ezra is the Son of God". Christians say: "The Messiah is the Son of God." That is what they utter in their mouths, conforming with those who were formerly unbelievers. May God assail them. How perverse they are.

APPENDIX B

Summary of the *Fatwās* of *Aḥmad b. Zakrī* and others, sought by *Qāḍī* al-ᶜAṣnūnī[131]

First Fatwā *of Ibn Zakrī,* muftī *of Tlemcen*

The question concerns demolition of an existing synagogue, to which the Jews have possessed the title for a long time, without there being any objection. *Dhimmīs* are forbidden to build new places of worship, but this does not mean it is an obligation to demolish those already built and possessed. Existing *kanīsas* should be left, even if new ones are forbidden. This applies to *dhimmīs* who have no pact. If they have a pact, and they move around within the lands of Islam, their pact remains, and they should be allowed to build a new *kanīsa.* The case of the Spanish Christians, which was the subject of Ibn al-Ḥājj's *fatwā*, is cited.

The protection (*dhimma*) given by the Muslims is one and indivisible, and its rights and disabilities are therefore portable from one part of the lands of Islam to another. Jews have an ancient *dhimma* in the lands of Islam, and are not known to make war against the Muslims, unlike the Christians of Spain, who were brought to the Maghrib to settle. To demolish the synagogues would be an injustice (*ẓulm*), and injustice towards *dhimmīs* is not permissible.

A citation from the *Jawāhir* of Ibn Shās:

> The pact of protection imposes duties on both parties. Upon the Muslims is the obligation to leave the *dhimmīs* in peace,

> and to protect their persons and property and not to interfere with their *kanīsa*s, their fermented liquors, or their pigs, so long as they keep them out of sight.

On the principles of enjoining what is right, and forbidding what is wrong:

1. He who does so must have knowledge of what is right and what is wrong [according to the law]. In regard to what is enjoined, there should be consensus that it is obligatory. What is prohibited should be forbidden (*ḥarām*), according to the consensus.

2. The result of forbidding something should not lead to a greater evil. In the case of the synagogues, it should be clear that in so far as their existence is an evil, demolishing them does not lead to a greater evil, such as the killing of *dhimmī*s and fighting among Muslims. It is agreed that killing *dhimmī*s, who have not broken the pact, is *ḥarām*. To kill those not guilty of breaking the pact would be an act of [culpable] homicide (*ḥirāba*).

3. The one who forbids something should know, or at least think it probable, that he will succeed.

Ibn Zakri's Second Fatwā (written after receiving al-Maghili's letter, etc.)

It is most likely that the Touat lands came into the possession of their owners through reclamation (*iḥyā'*), or the laying out of a settlement (*ikhtiṭāṭ*). It is unlikely that they were possessed either by force or by peace agreement. Hence there is no way that the synagogues there can be demolished, unless it can be shown that the Muslims gave the Jews the land on the understanding that they would not build synagogues on it. If this can be proved, the synagogues must be demolished. If they are demolished without such proof, it will be an act of tyranny and oppression. If the one who demolishes them denies the validity of imposing *jizya* and granting protection, he is denying the undisputed *ijmā*ᶜ, and his disbelief (*kufr*) will be clear.

First Fatwā *of al-Mawāsī,* muftī *of Fez*

Tuwat and other lands [of the Sahara] are part of the lands of Islam. No *kanīsa* should be allowed to stand there, unless it was stipulated as part of the *jizya* contract.

Second Fatwā *of al-Mawāsī*

Kanīsas already in existence should not be demolished, as they may result from an ancient privilege granted to the *dhimmīs*, unless it can be shown that the *dhimmīs* have transgressed by building such things, in which case the *kanīsas* may be demolished. Transgression is not to be presumed. In fact, the reverse is true since the people concerned are *dhimmīs*, who are humble and abased, and because no one has raised any objection to the synagogues over the years.

Fatwā *of Ibn Abī 'l-Barakāt, the* qaḍī al-jamā^{c}a *of Tlemcen*

Anyone with the least intelligence, who ponders on the facts of this case, will know that the synagogues may not be demolished, since warding off evil takes precedence over obtaining benefits. What evil could be greater than stirring up dissension and strife, which may lead to killing and plundering of property? If permission is given for such to happen it may spread from place to place, since evil people clutch at any straw to reach their wicked goals. How much more so, when the matter at issue is based in religion, and the hearts of those involved—even the scholars debating the issue—are filled with hatred! One should not go around looking for trouble. Scholars have kept silent on this matter for a long time and let the matter rest, since there is disagreement over it, and this can lead to strife. It is not permissible to destroy the synagogues. Indeed, it is *ḥarām* to do so. Precedence is important. Despite *ḥadīths*, scholars over the ages, in all times and places, have agreed in a contrary sense that the *Laylat al-qadr* should be celebrated on 27 Ramaḍān, and that one may write inscriptions on tombstones. Agreed practice can, therefore, override textual authority.

NOTES

Chapter 1

1. In Arabic: *qaṣr*, normally meaning "castle". For maps, or plans, of Tamantit and all of Touat, see Echallier (1972).
2. See Muḥammad al-Ṭayyib b. ᶜAbd al-Raḥmān al-Tamanṭīṭī, *al-Qawl al-basīṭ fī akhbār Tamanṭīṭ*, MS BNP, 6399, f. 2r.
3. See Oliel (1994), 132; also an image in Bakchine-Dumont (1975–76). Indeed, Jews were there much earlier; see Oliel (1994), 15–17.
4. The main cartographer was Abraham Cresques of Majorca. For a reproduction of part of this map, see Bovill (1968), front-piece; Timbuktu is spelled "Tenbuch".
5. See A.-G.-P. Martin (1908), 113–20.
6. In fact, according to Slouschz (1927), 344: "We are told of the Yehud Chaibar (the Rechab), a tribe of shepherds and agriculturalists, intrepid horsenen who at one time camped on the shores of the Red Sea, and who finally crossed the Sudan and penetrated to the farthest points of the Sahara".
7. See Meyer (1902), 113–36. These refugees from Iberia were called *Yahūd al-kabbūs*—"Jews of the hood". See also Hirschberg (1974), 407, quoting an anonymous contemporary author, who says that the ruler of Tlemcen provided financial incentives for Jews fleeing Spain to settle in his territory.
8. Meyer (1902), ix–x. The name Aln'Caoua is perhaps related to the Arabic *al-naqāwa*, meaning "purity" or "the choicest"; another brief account of him, with a transcription of his tombstone (he died in 1442), is given in a broader account of the Jewish community of Tlemcen, in Slouschz (1927), 324–29, where his name is spelled "(Al) Anquava". A later chapter of that book deals with Jews of the oases. See also Brunschvig (1940), 401.
9. Chouraqui (1985), 125; see also Rouche (1936), 280–86.
10. Jean-Léon l'Africain (Leo Africanus) (1956), ii, 333.

11. See al-ᶜUqbānī (1965–66), 170 (Arabic text).

Chapter 2

12. See art. *Djizja* in *EI* (2), ii, 559.
13. See Fattal (1958), 178.
14. See, with particular reference to Tlemcen, Shatzmiller (1978), 171–77.
15. There is a considerable literature on the social and economic realities of the life of *dhimmīs* in the lands of Islam, much of which focuses on the status and role of Jews. See, for example, Fattal (1958); Lewis (1984); and Bat Ye'or (1985), which contains a selection of translated documents. The book as a whole, however (including the documents), tends to dwell on negative aspects of the relationship between Muslims and *dhimmīs*. A partial antidote is in Goitein (1974).
16. On Khaybar there is a large article in *EI* (2), iv, 1137–43.
17. Text in al-Wansharīsī (1981), ii, 237–38; see also Tritton (1930).
18. *Kanīsa* basically means "temple", and is used to refer to either "church" or "synagogue"; see *EI* (2), iv, 545.
19. *Bīᶜa* may mean synagogue, but more often "church".
20. See al-ᶜUqbānī (1965–66), 171 (Arabic, p. 170).

Chapter 3

21. For his biography, see *EI* (2), v, 1165; *ALA* II, 20; Hunwick (1985), ch. 2.
22. Jean-Léon l'Africain (Leo Africanus) (1956), ii, 333.
23. See his *Tuḥfat al-nāẓir*, loc cit.
24. Ibid., 156–67 (Arabic text).
25. See al-Wansharīsī (1981), ii, 217–18. For a summary of *fatwās* in the *Miᶜyār*, dealing with *ahl al-dhimma*, see H. R. Idris (1974), 172–96.
26. Hirschberg (1974), 388.
27. Jean-Léon l'Africain (Leo Africanus) (1956), ii, 333. Meyer (1902) says there was a persecution of the Jews of Tlemcen af-

ter the Spanish capture of Oran in 1509. This may have been a reprisal for the assistance which a Jew is said to have given to the invaders; see al-Zayyānī (1979), 141–42. When the Spaniards captured Tlemcen in 1542, the Jews suffered at their hands, some 1,500 being killed or enslaved; see Hirschberg (1974), 444.

28. G.R. Crone, ed. & trans. (1937), 86.
29. al-Wansharīsī (1981), ii, 217. A *darb* is a lane branching off a main street, having gates at either end, or being a *cul-de-sac* with a gate at its open end. It thus constitutes a self-contained community; see Lane, *Arabic-English Lexicon* (London, 1863–93), iii, 866–67; Dozy, *Supplément aux dictionnaires arabes* (Leyde, 1881), ii, 429.
30. Harsh views of Jews by some Muslims even today reflect al-Maghīlī's attitude towards them. When many Palestinians began to sincerely soften their tone on Israelis, after many years of inter-population attacks and killings, the Palestinian "cleric", Sheik Ibrahim Mahdi, remarked: "We are waging this cruel war with the brothers of monkeys and pigs, the Jews and sons of Zion." Quoted in *The New York Times*, 15 December 2004, p. 1.
31. See Bibliothèque Générale et Archives, Rabat, Ms. no. Q683, 17ff.
32. Ed. Rābiḥ Būnār, Algiers, 1968, and compared with the edited text in Gwarzo's thesis in this translation.
33. Translations of this and all other portions of the Qur᾿ān are mainly based on [Muḥammad] Marmaduke Pickthall, *The Meaning of the Glorious Koran* (London: Allen and Unwin, 3rd impression, 1952).

Chapter 4

34. A phrase related to Qur᾿ān, 5:56: "And whoso takes God and His Messenger and those who believe as friends, then surely the party of God, they are the victorious ones."
35. A partial quotation of Qur᾿ān, 13:17.
36. The phrase "what your right hands possess" in the Qur᾿ān normally refers to slave women [concubines], captured in battle.

37. Qur'ān, 16:43; the "Remembrance" is a reference to prayer, "remembering" God.
38. I.e. ᶜIyāḍ b. Mūsā al-Yaḥṣubī, author of *al-Shifa' bi-taᶜrīf ḥuqūq al-Muṣṭafā.*
39. See Cairo edn., ed. ᶜAlī Muḥammad al-Bukhārī, Dār al-Kutub, 1977, vol. 2, 573.
40. Note by the editor of *al-Shifa'*: "related to him in family or marriage".
41. I.e. those who accompanied the Prophet in his move to Medina, and those who supported him there.
42. I.e. Anas b. Mālik, a young man given to the Prophet as a servant in Madina: see EI (2), i, 482.
43. After this another quotation from *al-Shifā'*, ii, 575.
44. *Sharīᶜa* refers to "Islamic law"; though not something that the Prophet himself created; rather legal rulings later based on what is in the Qur'ān and things the Prophet said on a similar matter.
45. The published text says: "and killed their fathers and sons".
46. A footnote to the text says: "By this, he means ᶜAbd Allāh b. Abī Sulūl, the leading hypocrite in Medina, whose son ᶜAbd Allāh was an exalted Muslim".
47. I.e. here ends the quotation from the *qāḍī ᶜIyāḍ*, p. 575 of *al-Shifa'*.
48. *Ustādh* is in modern Arabic the equivalent of "professor".
49. A long valley area in the extreme south of Morocco.
50. I.e. prepare himself to run, presumably by pulling up his robe to allow his legs easy fast movement.
51. I.e. jeweled necklaces.
52. The phrase in brackets is noted by the editor of the Arabic text as coming from a different manuscript copy.
53. Presumably Mālik b. Anas, initiator of the Mālkī *madh'hab* [law-school].
54. *Dhimmīs* are non-Muslims, living peacefully among Muslims. Non-Muslims outside of Muslim territories were people against whom war (*jihād*) was often made.
55. It is not entirely clear what the author aimed at, using Saḥnūn as the heading of a section. The meaning of *saḥnūn* in Egypt is "triumphant" or "successful".

56. The word *a*ᶜ*yād* (pl. of ᶜ*īd*) can also mean [religious] festivals.
57. ᶜUmar b. al-Khaṭṭāb was the second caliph after the death of the Prophet Muḥammad, directing the Muslim community 634–44 C.E.
58. mq. = *mithqāl*, a gold coin, weighing around 4.6 gr.
59. "Believers", i.e. Muslims.
60. Arabic: *qanāṭīr*—one *qinṭār* weighing between 44 and 256 kg. in different areas of the Arab world.
61. A *qibla* is the direction to which prayer is offered in a mosque, but here clearly refers to the praying place of Muslims plus that of any other religion.
62. I.e. the second follower of the Prophet—"Rightly-Guided" Caliph, *reg*. 634–44.
63. I.e. the region of modern Tunisia.

Chapter 4

64. Text: *al-ghalā*ᵓ*if*, a word not to be found in any dictionary of Classical Arabic. That spelling, hence, either reflects a local pronunciation of *khalā*ᵓ*if* (a plural form of *khalīfa*—"successor"—or in Tunisia "senior official"); or it is based on a misreading by a copyist. The word is spelled "*al-ghalā*ᵓ*if*" in the Fez lithograph edition of *al-Mi*ᶜ*yār al-mughrib* (of 1315/1897–98), which was also, apparently, the basis of the Beirut, 1981, edition.
65. See ᶜUmar Riḍā Kaḥḥāla, *Mu*ᶜ*jam al-mu*ᵓ*allifīn*, Beirut, n.d., x, 265; Aḥmad Bābā, *Nayl al-ibtihāj* (Cairo, 1351/1932–33), 329, calls him "a great memorizing jurisprudent, a cognizant writer" [*al-faqīh al-jalīl al-ḥāfiẓ, al-adīb al-muṭṭali*ᶜ].
66. See al-Wansharīsī, *al-Mi*ᶜ*yār al-mughrib*, ii, 235. Page numbers of this book are indicated in [ ], as quotations continue.
67. *Kanīsa*, which may mean "church" as well as "synagogue". Also *bay*ᶜ*a* is used for "church"; and for "synagogue" the word *shunūgha* or *shunūra* also exists.
68. *Idem.*, 236–37.
69. On Ibn Ḥibbān, see *EI* (2), i, 40.
70. See *GAL S* I, 166–67.

71. Several authors with this *nisba* wrote on *ḥadīth*. However, the most likely author referred to here is Abu Muḥammad al-Ḥusayn b. Mas[c]ūd; see *EI* (2), I, 893.
72. This is the title as given by Aḥmad Bābā in his *Kifāyat al-muḥtāj li-ma[c]rifat man laysa fī'l-Dībāj* (Rabat, 2000), ii, 23. In *al-Mi[c]yār al-mughrib*, ii, 236, it reads: *al-Injād fī ādāb al-jihād.*
73. p. 238, l. 1.
74. Ḥijr is another name for Madā'in Ṣāliḥ, a site of ruins in northwest Arabia. The area is associated in the Qur'ān with a people known as Thamūd, to whom was sent the prophet Ṣāliḥ. Ayla is a seaport at the north of the Gulf of [c]Aqaba. Dūmat al-Jandal is an oasis at the extreme northern end of the Arabian peninsula, also simply known as Dūma.
75. In the published text the word reads: *ajādīth*—an obvious error, writing *ḥā'* for *jīm.*
76. Abū Bakr Muḥammad b. al-Walīd al-Ṭurṭūshī (d. 1081) was an Andalusian Mālikī scholar; see *EI* (2), x, 739.
77. Ibn Ḥabīb's full name is [c]Abd al-Malik b. Ḥabīb b. Sulaymān b. Hārūn b. Janāhima b. [c]Abbās b. Mirdās al-Sulamī, also called Abū Marwān, an Andalusian Mālikī scholar (d. 238 or 239 A.H./ 852–54 C.E.); see Ibn Farḥūn, *al-Dībāj al-mudhahhab fī ma[c]rifat a[c]yān [c]ulamā' al-madh'hab* (Cairo, 1351/1932–33), pp. 154–56.
78. *al-Nawādir* by [c]Ubayd Allāh b. Abī Zayd al-Qayrawānī (d. 386/ 996); see *GAL S* I, 301–2.
79. Ibn al-Munāṣif's full name was Muḥammad b. [c]Īsā b. Muḥammad b. Aṣbagh b. Muḥammad b. Muḥammad b. Aṣbagh b. [c]Īsā b. Aṣbagh al-Azadī (d. 620/1223), but no writing with the title *Kitāb al-anjād* is attributed to him. This title may perhaps be an error for his *Kitāb al-ittiḥād fī abwāb al-jihād.*
80. *al-Mudawwana al-kubrā* of Saḥnūn [c]Abd al-Salām b. Sa[c]īd b. Ḥabīb al-Tanūkhī (d. 240/ 854); see *GAL S* I, 299.
81. Muḥammad b. Aḥmad b. [c]Abd al-[c]Azīz b. [c]Utba b. Ḥamīd b. [c]Utba al-Andalusī al-Mālikī (d. 869/ 1464–65), whose book is fully titled *al-Mustakhraja min al-asmā' al-masmū[c]a min Mālik b. Anas*, also known briefly as *al-Mustakhraja al-[c]utbiyya*; see [c]Umar Riḍā Kaḥḥāla, *Mu[c]jam al-mu'allifīn*, vii, 276; *GAL* I, 177.

82. Al-Fusṭāṭ was "the first city to be founded in Egypt by the Muslim conquerors"; see *EI* (2), ii, 957.
83. This wording differs from the earlier formulation.
84. I.e. no Jewish or Christian house of worship: synagogue or church.
85. ^{c}Alī b. ^{c}Abd Allāh b. Ibrāhīm al-Lakhmī (d. 1104), author of *Kitāb al-Nihāya wa 'l-Tamām fī ma^{c}rifar al-wathā$^{\supset}$iq wa 'l-aḥkām*; see *GAL* I, 383, *S* I, 661.
86. A Tunisian Mālikī (d. 1401); see *EI* (2), iii, 712; *GAL* II, 247.
87. The reference to Ibn Sahl may be to a 13th-century Andalusian poet of Jewish origin, converted to Islam, who also did service for governors of the region; see *EI* (2), iii, 925.
88. Abū ^{c}Umar Yūsuf b. ^{c}Abd Allāh b. Muḥammad b. ^{c}Abd al-Bārr al-Namarī al-Qurṭubī (d. 1071); *GAL* I, 367. His commentary on the *Muwaṭṭa$^{\supset}$* of Mālik b. Anas was abstracted into *al-Kāfī* (see *GAL S* I, 297.)
89. The *Jawāhir* of Ibn Shās was a work incorporated into the *Mukhtaṣar al-furū^{c}* of Jamāl al-Dīn Ibn al-Ḥājib; see *GAL S* I, 538 (viii).
90. *Kitāb al-dhakhīra fī 'l-furū^{c}* of Shihāb al-Dīn Abū 'l-^{c}Abbās Aḥmad b. Idrīs al-Qarāfī al-Ṣanhājī (d. 1285); see *GAL S* I, 665.
91. ^{c}Abd al-Raḥmān b. Muḥammad b. ^{c}Abd al-Raḥmān al-Mālikī Ibn ^{c}Askar (d. 1332); see *GAL* II, 163.
92. I.e. Khalīl b. Isḥāq al-Mālikī al-Miṣrī (d. 1374); see *EI* (2), iv, 964.
93. See *GAL S* II, 346, where the full title is given as *Tuḥfat al-nāẓir wa-ghunyat al-dhākir fī ḥifẓ al-sha$^{\supset}$ā^{c}ir wa- taghyīr al-manākir.*
94. An editor's note [on p. 248 of *al-Mi^{c}yār al-mughrib*] suggests that the text is corrupt at this point and should perhaps be restored as follows: "Whoever does not prevent them from doing that will receive [terrible] punishment." The text as it stands could be interpreted to mean that the threat of punishment on the Day of Judgment did not deter some ninety-eight Muslims from tolerating a situation in which Jews escaped some of the obligations laid upon them.
95. Lit. "May God heal the rift in Islam..."

96. See vol. 3 of this work (Beirut: Dār al-Fikr, 1978), 353.
97. The passage of the Qur'ān verse within [ ] is not in the *fatwā* text, which simply says "the [whole] verse".
98. *al-Mi*ᶜ*yār al-mughrib*, p. 250.
99. No doubt Abū Yūsuf Yaᶜqūb (reg. 1258–86).
100. A hilly region near the northern coast of Morocco.
101. The words *bī*ᶜ*a* and *kanīsa* both mean either "church" or "synagogue".
102. See *EI* (2), xi, 394, where Ẓāhiriyya is defined as: "A theologico-juridical school of mediaeval Islam, which may be situated, among *madh'hab*s as a whole, 'at the furthest limit of orthodoxy'."
103. Maᶜadd b. ᶜAdnān is said to have been in the ancestral family of the Prophet Muḥammad; see Khayr al-Dīn al-Ziriklī, *al-A*ᶜ*lām, Qāmūs al-tarājin* (3rd edn.), viii, 180.
104. I.e., the Day of Judgment.
105. Cf. Qur'ān, 9:29.
106. Reading *bi-*ᶜ*uqbihi*, rather than *bi-*ᶜ*aqabatin.*
107. A Tlemcen scholar (d. 1495); see al-Ziriklī, *al-A*ᶜ*lām, Qāmūs al-tarājim,* viii, 29; *GAL S* II, 352.
108. In the published text of al-Wansharīsī (1981), p. 253, the *nisba* reads al-Sh.s.ī; but for the correct *nisba* see *GAL* II, 241.

Chapter 5

109. Muḥammad b. ᶜAlī, Ibn ᶜAskar, *Dawḥat al-nāshir li-maḥāsin man kāna min al-Maghrib min ahl al-qarn al-*ᶜ*āshir*, Fez (litho.), 1309/1891–92, p. 95.
110. On the role of Jews in trans-Saharan trade, Dufourcq (1960), 141–42, notes: "C'est par les rapports entre les juiveries de Barcelone et de Majorque avec celles de Tlemcen et de Sijilmassa, que le contact le plus sûr et le plus direct était établi entre la Couronne d'Aragon et l'or du Soudan....la route d'or était aussi une route juive; et ce n'était là l'effet du hasard.....[Le] travail des métaux précieux, or et argent, a toujours été une prédilection des juifs en Afrique du Nord; et plus encore, le trafic même de ces métaux: le prêt, l'usure, ce que l'on appelle le commerce de l'argent; ils s'y

consacraient en même temps qu'au commerce des esclaves."

111. See Aḥmad Bābā, *Nayl al-Ibtihāj*, 331.
112. They named that location Elmina—"the mine"—which is still the name of the town, a westerly neighbor to Cape Coast city.
113. On this whole topic, see Magalhães-Godinho (1969), with detailed maps after p. 853.
114. Another argument in which the Jews were condemned was over their wearing clothes similar to the Muslims, and riding horses in a similar manner.
115. Published with an English translation by T.H. Baldwin (Beirut, 1932).
116. See Hunwick (1984).
117. Leo Africanus (1956), ii, 468.
118. See Haidara (1999).
119. Ibn ᶜAskar, *Dawḥat al-nāshir,* 96.
120. al-Maghīlī, *Taʾlīf fī mā yajib ᶜalā 'l-muslimīn*, 113.
121. Leo Africanus (1956), ii, 333.

Chapter 6

122. Leo Africanus (1956), ii, 436–37, who refers to Gourara as Tegorarin.
123. The number given of 500 households was out of a total of 13,000 households in the entire city. A total of 500 households might mean there was a Jewish population of around 3,000.
124. Davity (1660), 169.
125. See Hirschberg (1974), 441–42.
126. Written by A. Gavison in his *ᶜOmer ha-Shikeḥa*, and published in translation in Hirschberg (1974), 444.
127. See Chouraqui (1985), 532.
128. Park (1816), vol. i, 211.
129. See Haidara (1999), 114–21; and *Handlist of Manuscripts in the Centre de Documentation et de Recherches Historiques Ahmed Baba, Timbuktu,* vol. 5 (London: Al-Furqan Islamic Heritage Foundation, 1998). Relevant item numbers are to be found in Haidara's book. The book also shows the image of a Jewish rabbi

who was a merchant in Timbuktu in the nineteenth century; p. 20.

Appendix B

130. Such *fatwā* items are to be found in vol. 2 of Al-Wansharīsī (1981).

BIBLIOGRAPHY

1) *Source Materials*

Aḥmad Bābā. *Nayl al-Ibtihāj bi-tsṭrīz al-Dībāj*, on margins of Ibn Farḥūn, *al-Dībāj al-mudhahhab*. Cairo, 1351/1932–33.

ALA II—*Arabic Literature of Africa*, vol. 2, *The Writings of Central Sudanic Africa*, compiled by John O. Hunwick. Leiden: Brill, 1995.

Bargès, J.-J.-L. *Complément de l'histoire des Beni-Zeiyan, rois de Tlemcen, ouvrage du Cheikh Mohammed Abd'al-Djalil al-Tenessy*. Paris: Ernest Leroux, 1887.

Bū ᶜIyāḍ, Maḥmūd. *Taʾrīkh Banī Zayyān mulūk Tilimsān* [Drawn from the *Naẓm al-durr wa 'l-ᶜiqyān fī bayān sharf Banī Zayyān* of Muḥammad b. ᶜAbd Allāh al-Tanasī]. Algiers, 1985.

Crone, G.R., ed. & trans. (1937). *The Voyages of Cadamosto and other Documents on Western Africa in the Second Half of the Fifteenth Century*. London: Hakluyt Society.

Davity, Pierre (1660). *Description Générale de l'Afrique, Seconde Parti du Monde*, nouvelle édition revue, corrigé (*sic*) et augmenté (*sic*) . . . par Jean Baptiste de Rocoles. Paris.

EI (2)—*Encyclopaedia of Islam*, new edition, 11 vols. Leiden: Brill, 1960–2002.

GAL—*Geschichte der Araischen Literatur* by Carl Brockelmann. 2 vols. (2nd ed.), 1943–49, & 3 Supplementband, 1937–42. Leiden: Brill.

Hunwick, John O. (1999). *Timbuktu and the Songhay Empire: al-Saᶜdī's Taʾrīkh al-Sūdān down to 1613 and Other Contemporary Documents*. Leiden: Brill.

Idris, H.R. (1974). "Les tributaires en occident musulman médiéval d'après le '*Miᶜyār*' d'al-Wansharīsī". In Pierre Salmon, ed., *Mélanges d'Islamologie. Volume dédié à la mémoire d'Armand Abel*, pp. 172–96. Leiden: Brill.

Leo Africanus [al-Ḥasan b. al-Wazzān al-Zayyātī]:

Giovanni Leo Africanus (1550). *Delle descrittione dell'Africa*, in

G.B. Ramusio, *Delle navigationi e viaggi*, i, ff. 78–81r. Venice.
Jean-Léon l'Africain, trans. A. Epaulard (1956). *Description de l'Afrique*, 2 vols. Paris: Librairie d'Amérique et d'Orient Adrien-Maisonneuve.

Kaḥḥāla, ʿUmar Riḍā. *Muʿjam al-muʾallifīn*. Beirut, n.d.

al-Maghīlī, Muḥammad b. ʿAbd al-Karīm. *Taʾlīf fī mā yajib ʿalā 'l-muslimīn min ijtināb al-kuffār*. In Gwarzo (1972), 97–123.

Park, Mungo (1816). *Travels in the Interior Districts of Africa performed in the Years 1795, 1796, and 1797, with an Account of a Subsequent Mission in that Country in 1805*, new edition, 2 vols. London.

Pickthall, Marmaduke. *The Meaning of The Glorious Koran: An Explanatory Translation*. London: George Allen & Unwin, 1952.

Slouschz, Nahum (1927). *Travels in North Africa*. Philadelphia: Jewish Publication Society of America.

Al-ʿUqbānī, Muḥammad (1965–66). *Tuḥfat al-nāẓir wa-ghunyat al-dhākir fī ḥifẓ al-shaʿāʾir wa-taghyīr al-manākir*, ed. Ali Chennoufi, *Bull. d'Etudes Orientales* (Institut Français de Damas) 19.

al-Wansharīsī, Aḥmad b. Yaḥyā (1981). *al-Miʿyār al-mughrib ʿan fatāwī ʿahl Ifrīqiyā wa 'l-Andalus wa 'l-Maghrib*, 12 vols. Beirut: Dār al-Gharb al-Islāmī.

al-Zayyānī, Muḥammad b. Yūsuf (1979). *Dalīl al-ḥayrān wa-anīs al-sahrān fī akhbār madīnat Wahrān*, ed. Mahdī al-Būʿbdallī. Alger.

2) *Studies*

Bakchine-Dumont, Simonne (1975–76). "Les Juifs du Touat (XIVe et XVe siècles)", Mém. de Maîtrise, Université de Paris: Faculté des Lettres et Science Humaine.

Batran, ʿAbd-al-ʿAzīz ʿAbd-Allāh (1973). "A Contribution to the Biography of Shaikh Muḥammad ibn ʿAbd-al-Karīm ibn Muḥammad (ʿUmar-Aʿmar) al-Maghīlī, al-Tilimsānī", *J. African History* 14, no. 3:381–94.

Bat Yeʾor (1985). *The Dhimmi: Jews and Christians under Islam*. London and Toronto: Associated University Presses. (Trans. of *Le Dhimmi: Profil de l'opprimé en Orient et en Afrique du Nord depuis la conquête arabe*. Paris: Editions Anthropos, 1980.)

Beaumier, A. (1870). "Premier établissement des Israélites à Timbouk-ttou", *Bull. Soc. géogr. Paris*, pp. 345–70.

Bovill, E.W. (1968). *The Golden Trade of the Moors*, 2nd ed. London.

Brunschvig, Robert (1940). *La Berbérie Orientale sous les Ḥafṣides, des origines à la fin du XVe siècle.* Paris: Librairie d'Amérique et d'Orient, Adrien-Maisonneuve.

Capot-Rey, Robert (1953). *Le Sahara français*. Paris.

Chouraqui, André (1985). *Histoire des juifs en Afrique du Nord.* Paris: Hachette Littérature.

———— (1973), trans. Michael M. Bernet. *Between East and West: A History of the Jews of North Africa.* New York: Atheneum.

Crone, G.R. (1937), ed. *The Voyages of Cadamosto and other Documents on Western Africa in the Second Half of the Fifteenth Century.* London: Hakluyt Society, 2nd Series, lxxx.

Dufourq, Charles-Emmanuel (1966). *L'Espagne Catalane et le Maghrib aux XIII et XIV siècles.* Paris: Presses Universitaires de France.

Echallier, J-C. (1972). *Villages désertés et Structures Agraires Anciennes, du Touat-Gourara (Sahara Algérien).* Paris: A.M.G.

Fattal, Antoine (1958). *Le Statut légal des non-musulmans en pays d'Islam.* Beyrouth: Imprimerie Catholique.

Goitein, S. D. (1974). *Jews and Arabs: Their Contacts through the Ages*, 3rd ed. New York: Schocken Books.

Goldberg, Harvey E. (1990). *Jewish Life in Muslim Libya.* Chicago: University of Chicago Press.

Gwarzo, Hasan I. (1972). "The Life and Teachings of al-Maghīlī, with particular reference to the Saharan Jewish community", Ph.D. thesis, University of London.

Haidara, Ismael Diadié (1999). *Les Juifs à Tombouctou: receuil des sources écrites relatives au commerce juif à Tombouctou au XIX[e] siècle.* Bamako: Editions Donniya.

Hirschberg, H.Z. (1963). "The Problem of the Judaized Berbers", *J. African History* 4:323.

———. (1974). *A History of the Jews in North Africa.* Leiden: Brill.

Hunwick, John O. (1984). *Sharī[c]a in Songhay: The Replies of al-Maghīlī to the Questions of Askia al-Ḥājj Muḥammad.* Oxford University

Press [for the British Academy]: Fontes Historiae Africanae: Series Arabica, V.

———. (1985), "Al-Maghili and the Jews of Tuwat: the demise of a community", *Studia Islamica* 61:155–83.

———. (1991). "The rights of *dhimmīs* to maintain a place of worship: A 15th century *fatwā* from Tlemcen", *Al Qanṭara: Revista de Estudios Árabes*, 12, Fasc. 1, 133–55.

Lewis, Bernard (1984). *The Jews of Islam*. Princeton: Princeton University Press.

Magalhães-Godinho, Vitorino (1969). *L'Économie de l'Empire Portugais aux XVe et XVIe Siècles*. Paris: S.E.V.P.E.N.

Martin, A.-G.-P. (1908). *A la frontière du Maroc. Les oasis sahariennes (Gourara-Touat-Tidikelt)*. Alger.

Meyer, Abraham (1902). *Etude des moeurs actuelles des Israélites de Tlemçen*. Alger.

Oliel, Jacob (1994). *Les Juifs au Sahara: le Touat au Moyen Âge*. Paris: CNRS Éditions.

Rouche, Isaac (1936). "Un grand rabbin à Tlemçen au XVe siècle", *Bulletin de la Société de Géographie et Archéologie d'Oran* 57:280–86.

Shatzmiller, Maya (1978). "Les Juifs de Tlemçen au XIVe siècle", *Revue des Études juives* 137:171–77.

Stillman, Norman (1979). *The Jews of Arab Lands: A History and Source Book*. Philadelphia: Jewish Publication Society of America.

Tritton, A. S. (1930). *The Caliphs and Their Non-Muslim Subjects: A Critical Study of the Covenant of ^{c}Umar*. London: F. Cass.

Ward, Seth. "Construction and Repair of Churches and Synagogues in Islamic Law: A Treatise by Taqī al-Dīn ^{c}Alī b. ^{c}Abd al-Kāfī al-Subkī", Ph. D. thesis, Yale University, 1984.

Vajda. (1962). "Un traité <Adversos Judaeos>: *Aḥkām ahl al-dhimma* du Ṣayḫ Muḥammad b. ^{c}Abd al-Karīm al-Maghīlī", in *Études d'orientalisme dédiées à la mémoire de Lévi-Provençal,* pp. 805–813. Paris.

INDEX

NOTE: the titles *al-Ḥājj*, *Qāḍī*, and *Shaykh* are not considered in alphabetization; nor is al- or b.= *ibn*.

ᶜAbd al-Malik, 42
al-ᶜAbdūsī (see Abū 'l-Qāsim al-ᶜAbdūsī)
Abū ᶜAbd Allāh Muḥammad, ruler of Tlemcen 66
Abū ᶜAbd Allāh Sīdī Muḥammad b. Yūsuf al-Sanūsī (see Muḥammad b. Yūsuf al-Sanūsī)
Abū Dāwūd 36
Shaykh Abū 'l-Ḥasan al-Ashᶜarī 27
Shaykh Abū 'l-Ḥasan al-Maghribī 41, 43
Abū ᶜInān, Sultan of Fez 29
Abū Mahdī ᶜĪsā b. Aḥmad al-Māwasī, *muftī* of Fez 34
Shaykh Abū Muḥammad [ᶜAbd Allāh] b. Abī Zayd al-Qayrawānī 44
Abū 'l-Qāsim al-ᶜAbdūsī 54, 55, 57
Abū ᶜUbayd Qāsim b. Sallām 36
Shaykh Abū 'l-Walīd al-Ṭurṭūshī 22, 40
Abū Yaᶜla al-Mawṣilī 37
Abū Zakariyyaᵓ Yaḥyā b. ᶜAbd Allāh b. Abī 'l-Barakāt, *qāḍī 'l-jamāᶜa* of Tlemcen 34, 73
Aḥkām of Ibn Ziyād 50
Aḥmad ibn Ḥanbal 56
Aḥmad b. Muḥammad, known as Ibn Zakrī, *muftī* of Tlemcen 11, 34, 71
Aḥmad b. Yaḥyā al-Wansharīsī 34–35
Algeria 1, 66–67
Almohads 2
Almoravids 1, 43
Anas [b. Mālik] 17
Andalusia 34, 43, 62, 66
Antonius Malfante, a Genoese merchant 2, 12
Aragon 2
Arguin 62
Askiya *al-Ḥājj* Muḥammad vii, 63–64
Qāḍī al-ᶜAṣnūnī 12, 14, 33–34, 71

Al-Baghawī 36
Balearic Islands 2
Banū Ṣubayḥ 18
Basra 40
Bougie 66
Byzantines 5, 65

Caliph ᶜUmar b. ᶜAbd al-ᶜAzīz (see ᶜUmar b. ᶜAbd al-ᶜAzīz)
Caliph ᶜUmar b. al-Khaṭṭāb 7–8, 24, 27–28, 36–37
Capot-Rey, the French traveler 1
Castille 2
Centre de Documentation et de Recherches Historiques [CEDRAB] 67
Charles V of Aragon 1
Cordova 50, 57

Darᶜa (see also Dra) 18, 28
Dhakhīra of al-Qarāfī 52
Dra (see also Darᶜa) 1, 2

Egypt 66
Ephraim Aln'Caoua 3

Fatwā of al-ᶜAbdūsī 54
Fez 2, 67
Figuig 2
al-Figīgī, Muḥammad b. ᶜAbd al-Jabbār 33
al-Fusṭāṭ 41, 44–45

Gao, the 'capital' of the Songhay empire 1, 63–64
al-Ghazālī 56
Gourara 64–65

Ḥafṣids 2
al-Ḥasan al-Baṣrī 41
Ḥassan b. Mālik 40

Ibn ᶜAbbās 36, 39–40, 42
Ibn ᶜArafa 48–50
Ibn ᶜAskar 52–53, 61, 64
Ibn Badrān 37, 40, 57
Ibn *al-Ḥājj* al-Fāsī 33
Ibn Ghāzī 13
Ibn Ḥabīb 37, 43, 45, 48
Ibn Ḥazm 29, 57
Ibn Ḥibbān 36–37, 39
Ibn Kināna 46
Ibn al-Mājishūn 37, 43, 48
Ibn al-Munāṣif 36, 44, 56
Ibn al-Mundhir 56
Ibn al-Qāsim 41–42, 45–47, 49, 54
Ibn Rushd 44–47
Ibn Sahl 51, 57
Ibn Yūnus 47
Ibn Zakrī, *muftī* of Tlemcen 11, 34, 71
Ibrāhīm al-Maṣmūdī 18
Ifrīkīyā 28
al-Injād fī abwāb al-jihād of Ibn al-Munāṣif 36

al-Jamᶜ wa'l-furūq, of al-Qarāfī 28
Jawāhir of Ibn Shās 52, 71
Jerusalem 1, 3, 65
jihad 26, 57
jizya 5, 11, 14, 24–26, 28, 34, 43, 48, 52–54, 56–58, 61, 72–73

Kāfī of Abū ᶜUmar b. ᶜAbd al-Bārr 51
Kano 2, 63
Khaybar 7, 13, 43
al-Khazrajī, the *qāḍī* of Bādis and elsewhere in Al-Rīf 56
Kitāb al-anjād of Ibn al-Munāṣif 44
Kitāb al-amwāʾ 36
Koufa 40

al-Lakhmī 46–50, 53
Leo Africanus 3, 12, 63, 65–66
Libya 66

Maᶜadd b. ᶜAdnān 58
al-Madīna (see also Medina) 39
al-Maghīlī, Muḥammad b. ᶜAbd al-Karīm 11, 14, 59
Maḥmūd b. ᶜUmar, the *qāḍī* of Timbuktu 64
Majorca 2
Mālik b. Anas 37
Marātib al-Ijmāᶜ of Ibn al-Ẓāhirī 57
Marinids 2, 56
Al-Māwardī 56
al-Mawāsī the *muftī* of Fez 34, 73
Mecca 65
Medina 7, 65
al-Miᶜyār al-mughrib ᶜan fatāwī ᶜulamāʾ Ifrīqiyā wa 'l-Andalus wa 'l-Maghrib 34
al-Mudawwana 41–42, 44–51, 53, 55, 57
Morocco 2, 62, 67
Muḥammad, the Prophet 7, 13,

16–22, 24–27, 30, 36, 44, 46, 65
Muḥammad b. ᶜAbd al-Jabbār al-Figīgī 33
Muḥammad b. ᶜAbd al-Jalīl al-Tanasī 12, 35, 39, 60–63
Muḥammad b. ᶜAbd al-Karīm al-Maghīlī 11, 14, 59
Muḥammad b. Qāsim al-Anṣārī, known as al-Raṣṣāᶜ, *qāḍī 'l-jamāᶜa* and *muftī* of Tunis 34
Muḥammad Rumfa, Sultan of Kano 63
Qāḍī Muḥammad al-ᶜUqbānī 3, 11–12, 53
Muḥammad b. Yūsuf al-Sanūsī 58–59
Mukhtaṣar [of Abū 'l-Ḥasan al-Qaddūri] 56
Mungo Park 67
al-Mustakhraja of al-ᶜUtbī 44

al-Nawādir 44
Nawāzil of Ibn Sahl 50
Nebuchadnezzar 65

Oasis of Khaybar 7
Oran 66
Ottoman sailors 66

Al-Qarāfī 22, 28, 53

Romans 65

Sālim b. ᶜAbd Allāh 37
al-Shāfiᶜī 56
Sicily 65
Sīdī Hibat Allāh 18
Sijilmasa 1–2
Songhay vii, 63–64, 67
Spaniards 66–67

Tāfilālt 28
Tāj al-Dīn fī mā yajib ᶜalā 'l-mulūk 63
Tamantit vii, 1–3, 11–12, 33–35, 59–61, 63–65
al-Ṭāᵓūs al-Yamanī 41
Tawḍīḥ 52
Tījūrārīn 28
Timbuktu 1, 62–64, 67
Tlemcen 1–3, 11–12, 18, 28, 34–35, 62, 64–67, 71, 73
Touat vii, 1–3, 12, 14, 28, 33, 35, 52–53, 62, 64–65, 72
Tripoli 66
Tuggourt 2
Tuḥfat al-nāẓir fitaghyīr al-manākir 53
Tunis 2, 34, 42–43, 54
Tunisia 2, 66

ᶜUmar b. al-Khaṭṭāb 7–8, 24, 27–28, 36–37
ᶜUmar b. ᶜAbd al-ᶜAzīz 40, 50
ᶜUmda of Ibn ᶜAskar al-Baghdādī 52
al-ᶜUtbiyya 47
al-ᶜUqbānī 3, 11–12, 53

al-Wāḍiḥa of Ibn Ḥabīb 43, 45, 47–51
Walata 2, 62, 67
Warghla 2

Yūsuf b. Yaᶜqūb b. ᶜAbd al-Ḥaqq al-Marīnī 56
Yūsuf b. Tāshfīn 1

Zayyānids 2, 12

www.ingramcontent.com/pod-product-compliance
Lightning Source LLC
Chambersburg PA
CBHW031643170426
43195CB00035B/564
9781558763463